TEACHER'S GUIDE FOR
Discovering the world through DEBATE
third edition

TEACHER'S GUIDE FOR

Discovering the world through DEBATE
third edition

Nancy E. Claxton, Ed.D.

INTERNATIONAL DEBATE EDUCATION ASSOCIATION

NEW YORK • AMSTERDAM • BRUSSELS

Published by
the International Debate Education Association

international debate education association

Copyright © 2006 by
the International Debate Education Association

All rights reserved. No part of this publication may be reproduced or transmitted in any form or by any means, electronic or mechanical, including photocopy, or any information storage and retrieval system, without permission from the publisher.

For permission to reproduce in whole or in part, please contact: idea@idebate.org

Library of Congress Cataloging-in-Publication Data

Claxton, Nancy E.
Teacher's guide for discovering the world through debate 3rd ed./ Nancy E. Claxton
-- 1st ed.
    p. cm.
 ISBN-10: 1-932716-26-2 (alk. paper)
 ISBN-13: 978-1-932716-26-9.
 1. Debates and debating. I. Teacher's guide for discovering the world through debate.
  PN4181.D75 2006
  808.5'3--dc22

                2006014160

Design by Marcel R. Claxton

Printed in the USA

IDEBATE Press Books

Contents

INTRODUCTION	viii
Preparation	viii
Content of the Textbook	ix
The Course	x
Course Requirements	x
Terminal Course Objectives (TCOs)	x
WEEKLY TOPIC OUTLINE	xiii
WEEK 1	1
OBJECTIVES	1
CHAPTER FOCUS	1
LESSON	1
Warm-up	1
Karl Popper Debate and the Public Sphere (TCO A)	2
The Debate Club in the School Community (TCO Y)	5
Wrap-up	6
ADDITIONAL ACTIVITIES	7
WEEK 2	8
OBJECTIVES	8
CHAPTER FOCUS	8
LESSON	8
Warm-up	8
The Structure of Argument (TCOs B & C)	8
Claims and Propositions (TCO D)	10
Wrap-up	14
WEEK 3	15
OBJECTIVES	15
CHAPTER FOCUS	15
LESSON	15
Warm-up	15
Types of Evidence (TCOs E and F)	15
Warrants (TCOs G & H)	18
Wrap-up	26
WEEK 4	27
OBJECTIVES	27
CHAPTER FOCUS	27
LESSON	27
Warm-up	27
The Quality of Arguments (TCOs I and J)	27
Fallacies	29
Developing Research Skills (TCO R)	31
Wrap-up	33
ADDITIONAL ACTIVITIES	34
WEEK 5	35
OBJECTIVES	35
CHAPTER FOCUS	35

LESSON	35
Warm-up	35
The Karl Popper Debate Format (TCO K & U)	36
Wrap-up	38
ADDITIONAL ACTIVITIES	38
WEEK 6	**39**
OBJECTIVES	39
CHAPTER FOCUS	39
LESSON	39
Warm-up	39
Constructing Arguments about Claims of Cause and Effect (TCOs M & L)	39
Wrap-up	42
WEEK 7	**43**
OBJECTIVES	43
CHAPTER FOCUS	43
LESSON	43
Warm-up	43
Constructive Arguments about Claims of Value (TCOs L, N, & O)	43
Wrap-up	46
WEEK 8	**47**
OBJECTIVES	47
CHAPTER FOCUS	47
LESSON	47
Warm-up	47
Arguing about Simple Policy Propositions (TCOs L & P)	47
Constructing Arguments to Support a Claim of Comparative Policy	50
Wrap-up	52
WEEK 9	**53**
OBJECTIVES	53
CHAPTER FOCUS	53
LESSON	53
Warm-up	53
Refutation and Rebuttals (TCO Q)	54
Cross-examination (TCOs S & T)	56
Wrap-up	58
ADDITIONAL ACTIVITIES	58
WEEK 10	**59**
OBJECTIVES	59
CHAPTER FOCUS	59
LESSON	59
Warm-up	59
Arrangement, Style, and Delivery (TCO U & V)	59
Debating in an International Setting (TCO X)	62
Wrap-up	63
ADDITIONAL ACTIVITIES	63
WEEK 11	**64**
OBJECTIVES	64
CHAPTER FOCUS	64

PREPARATION	64
LESSON	64
Warm-up	64
Judging Debates (TCO W)	64
Wrap-up	67
ADDITIONAL ACTIVITIES	67

WEEK 12   68
OBJECTIVES	68
LESSON	68
Warm-up	68
Final Class Session	68
Wrap-up	70

APPENDIX
COURSE SYLLABUS	71

WORKSHEETS
1. DISTINGUISHING BETWEEN CLAIMS, PROPOSITIONS, AND EVIDENCE	74
2. KARL POPPER QUOTES	76
3. GROUP DISCUSSION QUESTIONS FOR KARL POPPER DEBATE TRANSCRIPT AND COMMENTARY READING	78
4. ARGUING AND REFUTING CAUSAL RELATIONSHIPS	82
5. BUILDING A CASE FOR AND AGAINST A SIMPLE VALUE PROPOSITION	83
6. BUILDING A CASE FOR A COMPARATIVE VALUE PROPOSITION - FACT SHEET	86
7. ARGUMENT FLOW SHEET	90
8. KARL POPPER DEBATE BALLOT AND SCORING RUBRIC	91

Introduction

This *Teacher's Guide* serves as a manual for using *Discovering the World through Debate*, third edition. It provides lesson plans for a 12-week course, with 180 minutes of classroom instruction weekly. Activities vary, but all are designed to help students understand debate on a theoretical and practical level.

PREPARATION

Please read the introduction and review the Weekly Topic Outline (p. xiii) to get an overview of how the course is organized and what is expected from the students. Consult the Weekly Topic Outline as you plan your lessons, and remember to read the appropriate sections of the textbook because this guide follows the textbook closely. The guide explains techniques and concepts from the textbook and highlights the key points of each chapter, but it does not replicate the comprehensive information in the textbook.

The *Teacher's Guide* promotes effective teaching through the use of myriad instructional techniques that support effective teaching. Most important, it provides a framework that encourages and nurtures your individual and professional creativity, experience, and insights. While this manual offers a fairly rigid teaching syllabus, we encourage you to structure and configure the content in a way consistent with your professional experience and the needs of your students. Remember to utilize real world examples and applications in your presentations and to provide meaningful feedback to your students based on your own experience with debate. Debate is dynamic and exciting, and thus you should feel free to modify the lesson plans provided or to develop your own.

The *Teacher's Guide* presents material in a variety of instructional approaches and always strives to foster best teaching practices. As you use this manual, follow these general practices:

1. Post the learning objectives for each training session in an accessible place. Posting objectives and referring to them throughout the lesson shows the students that the lesson is structured and carefully thought out. Knowing what the lesson will accomplish makes the students more comfortable in embarking on new approaches and unfamiliar material.

2. Regularly review the Terminal Core Objectives (TCOs) of the course with your students. This review assures them that each session is furthering the goal of the course. Each lesson plan lists the TCOs associated with that session.

3. Regularly assess the progress of your students. Assessment is the key to measuring the students' understanding of the new material. In this course, assessment is based on in-class participation in projects, activities, and debates. There are no out-of-class work expectations, such as papers or exams, because this is a practical course.

4. Start each session with a Warm-up or review of the prior session's objectives and activities. Then introduce the objectives for the current week and briefly explain how these objectives will be met.

5. End each session with a 3 to 5 minute Wrap-up, during which you review the objectives for that lesson and summarize how those objectives were met. You should also answer any remaining questions at this time.

However you choose to use this guide, we hope that it will help you utilize *Discovering the World through Debate* to bring debate alive. Get ready, get set, debate!

CONTENT OF THE TEXTBOOK

The *Discovering the World through Debate*, third edition, is divided into three parts. Part I introduces argumentation theory, focusing on those concepts of argumentation most useful to debaters. Part II discusses constructing arguments in ways appropriate for Karl Popper debate. It begins with a chapter explaining the Karl Popper format and then presents chapters on supporting and opposing propositions of cause and effect, value, and policy. Finally, Part III discusses a variety of debating skills—research, cross-examination, style, and delivery—and concludes with chapters on judging and international debating.

Although they overlap, the three parts of this book are also independent. You can use them in the order presented or in some other order, as you see fit. For instance, you may want to begin with Part II, teaching students the details of the Karl Popper debate format and the methods of constructing cases for and against a proposition. You might then move to Part III to refine students' skills in various aspects of debate and end with Part I and a consideration of how the theory of argumentation informs argument construction and debating skills.

This edition of *Discovering the World through Debate* is a substantial revision of the first two editions. The first two editions of this textbook served the International Debate Education Association (IDEA) community well during the first decade of its development. In recent years, IDEA has introduced more complex kinds of resolutions so that students can learn more advanced forms of debate. This edition is designed to meet the needs of participants who are ready to progress to new and more complex levels of argumentation and debate. All of Part I is entirely new and all but one chapter in Part II is new; the chapters in Part III are substantial revisions of materials presented in the first and second editions.

Note: The examples used in this guide do not represent the views held by the Open Society Institute or the authors of the text.

THE COURSE

The *Teacher's Guide* is keyed to *Discovering the World through Debate*, third edition, which is required reading for the course. The textbook is an introduction to argumentation and to the practical skills needed for debate, specifically using the Karl Popper format. The three broad topics covered are argumentation theory, argument construction, and debating skills.

Course Requirements

We have organized the course around six basic requirements:

1. Assigned Readings—Each lesson will include assigned readings from *Discovering the World through Debate*, third edition. Students should complete the readings before the session so that they can gain the maximum benefit from the lesson.

2. Debate Analysis—Students will analyze at least two Karl Popper debates using an argument flow sheet.

3. Debate Design and Delivery—Students will design and deliver a structured debate and will also assume the various roles that debaters take on in actual debates.

4. In-Class Projects—In-class projects and impromptu debate sessions will help students learn how debates are structured and how to participate in debates. They will also help students understand the demands and expectations of debate judges.

5. Class Participation—Because this is a practical course, participants are expected to actively participate in debates and in-class discussions and activities.

6. Assessment—Students will be assessed on participation and in debate performance as individuals and as part of a team. Students are expected to attend class regularly.

Terminal Course Objectives (TCOs)

Terminal Course Objectives (TCOs) are the main learning objectives that the students taking the course should meet. The following objectives explain what they should know or be able to do by the end of the course:

A. Given the important elements of argument, define and properly utilize claims, evidence, warrants, and reservations.

B. Given a model to simulate a theoretical argument, appropriately chart out an argument to ensure all necessary parts are included.

C. Given evidence and a claim, assess the structure of an argument as simple, convergent, or independent.

D. Given a claim or proposition, evaluate whether it is a claim of definition, description, relationship, or evaluation.

E. Given evidence for a claim, categorize it as reality-based or preference-based or a combination of reality- and preference-based.

F. Given a value hierarchy, categorize whether the evidence is organized according to quantity, quality, order, existent, essence, or person.

G. Given an argumentative warrant, categorize it as example, analogy, causal warrant, authority, principle, incompatibility, or disassociation, or some combination of these warrants, by its use in an argument.

H. Given a criterion for logical assessment of an argument, assess if the standards of acceptability, relevance, and sufficiency are met.

I. Given a fallacy, identify how it fails to meet a criterion for logical assessment of an argument.

J. Given an example of a Karl Popper debate, devise or analyze a debate within the established format.

K. Given the claim of an argument, classify it as a cause-and-effect, value, or policy claim.

L. Given an argument to defend or attack, apply the five steps of refutation to a debate.

M. Given a debate topic, develop a plan to generate general and specific knowledge.

N. Given an opportunity to cross-examine the other team, question the opponent appropriately, flexibly, pointedly, specifically, and with innovation when necessary.

O. Given the opportunity to respond to cross-examination, respond carefully, succinctly, and appropriately, and if necessary, admit lack of knowledge.

P. Given a debate topic, arrange ideas by topic, time and history, problem and solution, or relationship.

Q. Given components and elements of style, exhibit and identify those related to the use of language, use of voice, speech style, and nonverbal style.

R. Given the opportunity to serve as a debate judge, understand the criteria for judging and ethically carry out the duties and tasks required.

S. Given the requirements of debating internationally, understand and exhibit the demands required of debaters arguing within the confines of foreign languages, countries, and customs.

T. Given the benefits of debate clubs in schools, devise ways to foster support, inclusion, and cooperation.

U. Given an opportunity to read or hear a debate, flow the debate using appropriate columns and references.

The TCOs are keyed to the activities in each lesson.

Weekly Topic Outline

WEEK 1

- Introductions and preview of class expectations
- Distribute syllabus
- Debate in personal, technical, and public spheres
- Preview of important features of public debate
- Karl Popper debate as a form of public argument
- The benefits of debate as an educational activity
- The composition of a debate club
- Fostering a spirit of inclusion and cooperation
- Club space
- Club meetings and working sessions
- Club leadership and organization
- Recruitment and retention
- The role of coaches, teachers, and parents

Reading Assignment: *Discovering the World through Debate (DTW)* chapters 1 and 17

WEEK 2

- The elements of argument
- Structure of an argument
  - ✓ Simple arguments
  - ✓ Convergent arguments
  - ✓ Independent arguments
- Distinguishing claims and propositions
- Types of claims and propositions

- ✓ Propositions of definition
- ✓ Propositions of description
- ✓ Propositions of relationship
- ✓ Propositions of evaluation
- ❑ The centrality of values in claims and propositions

Reading Assignment: *DTW* chapters 2 and 3

WEEK 3

- ❑ Categories of evidence
  - ✓ Facts
  - ✓ Theories
  - ✓ Presumptions
- ❑ Values
- ❑ Value hierarchies
- ❑ Value categories
- ❑ Argumentative warrants
  - ✓ Argument by example
  - ✓ Argument by analogy
  - ✓ Argument by causality
  - ✓ Argument by authority
  - ✓ Principle
  - ✓ Incompatibility
  - ✓ Disassociation

Reading Assignment: *DTW* chapters 4 and 5

WEEK 4

- ❑ Criteria for logical assessment of arguments

- ✓ The standard of acceptability
- ✓ The standard of relevance
- ✓ The standard of sufficiency
- ❏ Three basic fallacies and argument adequacy
- ❏ Fallacies related to language
  - ✓ Problematic premises
  - ✓ Irrelevant reasons
  - ✓ Hasty conclusions
- ❏ Fallacies related to language
- ❏ The importance of research
- ❏ The research process and its stages
  - ✓ Phase 1: General knowledge
    - ✦ Locate background information
    - ✦ Accumulate general knowledge
    - ✦ Determine the general issues
    - ✦ Review and research footnotes and bibliographies
  - ✓ Phase 2: Specific knowledge
    - ✦ Outline the vital specific issues
    - ✦ Brainstorm concepts
    - ✦ Accumulate research on specific issues
    - ✦ Review and research footnotes and bibliographies
- ❏ Researching from source material

Reading Assignment: *DTW* chapters 6 and 12

WEEK 5

- ❏ Introduction to Karl Popper debate format
- ❏ The sections of Karl Popper debate

- ❏ The Karl Popper debate format
    - ✓ Affirmative Constructive
    - ✓ Cross-examination
    - ✓ Negative Constructive
    - ✓ Cross-examination
    - ✓ First Affirmative Rebuttal
    - ✓ Cross-examination
    - ✓ First Negative Rebuttal
    - ✓ Final Affirmative Rebuttal
    - ✓ Final Negative Rebuttal
- ❏ Team format
- ❏ The roles of team members
- ❏ Preparation time

Reading Assignment: *DTW* chapter 7

WEEK 6

- ❏ Arguing about cause and effect
- ❏ Theoretical elements of causal reasoning
- ❏ Methods used to refute and support causal reasoning
    - ✓ Method of agreement
    - ✓ Method of difference
    - ✓ Method of correlation
- ❏ Types of causal argument
    - ✓ Necessary causal argument
    - ✓ Sufficient causal argument
    - ✓ Contributory causal argument
    - ✓ Intervening and counteracting causes

- ❏ Constructing arguments to support a cause-and-effect relationship
    - ✓ Describing features of the cause
    - ✓ Demonstrating the effect
    - ✓ Demonstrating a causal relationship
- ❏ Constructing arguments to oppose a cause-and-effect relationship

Reading Assignment: *DTW* chapter 8

WEEK 7

- ❏ Constructing an argument to support a simple value proposition
- ❏ Combining claims to support a simple value proposition
- ❏ Constructing an argument for a comparative value proposition
- ❏ Combining claims to support a comparative value proposition
- ❏ Constructing an argument to oppose value propositions
    - ✓ Arguments with respect to description
    - ✓ Arguments with respect to causal relationships
    - ✓ Arguments with respect to evaluation
- ❏ Developing a coherent negative case

Reading Assignment: *DTW* chapter 9

WEEK 8

- ❏ Policy claims
- ❏ The role of values in policy claims
- ❏ Constructing arguments about simple policy propositions
    - ✓ A need-plan-benefits strategy
        - ✦ The need
        - ✦ The plan
        - ✦ The benefits

- ✦ The strategy
- ❑ Negative strategies for debating about policies
    - ✓ Concept of presumption
    - ✓ Defending the status quo
    - ✓ Defending a policy other than the status quo
    - ✓ Attacking the plan
- ❑ Constructing arguments to support a claim of comparative policy
    - ✓ Stance of the affirmative
    - ✓ Conceptualizing the case
    - ✓ Constructing the affirmative plan
    - ✓ Constructing the advantages
- ❑ Constructing arguments against the propositions of comparative policies
    - ✓ Stance of the negative
    - ✓ Constructing the negative case

Reading Assignment: *DTW* chapter 10

WEEK 9

- ❑ Refutation
- ❑ Rebuttals
    - ✓ Summarizing arguments
    - ✓ Identifying vital issues
    - ✓ Making choices
    - ✓ Weigh implications
- ❑ Cross-examination ground rules
- ❑ Purposes of cross-examination
    - ✓ Obtain information
    - ✓ Clarify an argument for the debater

- ✓ Clarify an argument for the judge
- ✓ Commit a debater to a position
- ✓ Elicit information useful in building an argument
- ✓ Establish a plan of refutation
- ✓ Identify inadequacies in an argument
- ✓ Undermine the opponent's credibility
- ✓ Enhance your own impression and credibility
- ✓ Prepare for constructive arguments
- ❑ Advice for the questioner and respondent
- ❑ General advice for cross-examination

Reading Assignment: *DTW* chapters 11 and 13

WEEK 10

- ❑ Arrangement of arguments
  - ✓ Arranging by topic
  - ✓ Arranging by time/history
  - ✓ Arranging by problem-solution
  - ✓ Arranging by relationship
- ❑ Style and delivery
  - ✓ Components of style
  - ✓ Elements of style
  - ✓ Nonverbal style
- ❑ Cultural diversity while debating in an international setting
- ❑ Practical difficulties of international debating

Reading Assignment: *DTW* chapters 14 and 16

WEEK 11

❑ Responsibilities of the judge

- ✓ Focus on the debate
- ✓ Understand the criteria for judging
- ✓ Make independent decisions
- ✓ Explain decisions
- ✓ Maintain an ethical means of decision making
- ✓ Undertake practical tasks

❑ Judge ballots

Reading Assignment: *DTW chapter 15*

WEEK 12

❑ Debate exercise

Week 1

OBJECTIVES

Students will be able to do the following:

1. Understand the objectives of the course and relate their previous experience with debate to these goals

2. Understand that debate and argumentation occur in three distinct yet overlapping spheres: the personal, the technical, and the public

3. Understand that the important features of debate in the public sphere include audience, evidence, reason, and language

4. Understand the goals of the Karl Popper debate format

5. Understand the importance of debaters thinking as a team rather than as individuals

6. Understand the key elements in forming a successful, on-going debate club

7. Understand the role coaches and parents play in a debate club

CHAPTER FOCUS

DTW chapters 1 and 17

LESSON

Warm-up

1. Introduce yourself. Give your current position and describe your past experience in debate—as a debater, trainer, coach, judge, or observer. Ask the students to introduce themselves and offer some background: why they are taking this course and what their experience with debate has been. *(10–15 minutes)*

2. Distribute the syllabus (p. 71) and discuss. Answer any questions that may arise. Remind the students that they must complete the reading assignment before each week's session begins. *(10–15 minutes)*

> **KEY POINTS**
>
> - Students probably have experience with debate—even if only informally in daily conversation. This course will give them the knowledge and skills to engage in formal debate.
>
> - The course provides practical experience in three main areas: argumentation for debaters, construction of arguments in the Karl Popper debate format, and development of debate skills.
>
> - Completing the reading assignments before the week's lessons helps the class progress smoothly and allows maximum opportunity for students to benefit from in-class time.

3. Refer to this week's objectives and briefly preview the lesson with the students. *(3–5 minutes)*

KARL POPPER DEBATE AND THE PUBLIC SPHERE (TCO A)

1. Teach Activity #8: "Issue Flexibility Inventory" (*DTW* p. 213). After the students have completed the activity, lead a discussion about the variety of topics that are debatable and help students develop criteria for debatability. Explain that formal debate can take many forms and that in this course they will focus on one—the Karl Popper debate format. *(15–20 minutes)*

2. Discuss the three spheres of debate: personal, technical, and public. *(7 minutes)*

> **KEY POINTS**
>
> - Each sphere has different standards for good arguments.
>
> - Personal sphere debates include arguments between family members or friends over personal matters.
>
> - Technical sphere debates usually involve participants who share common areas of expertise. Debaters share extensive knowledge of their subject and a precise vocabulary. Debates in this sphere can also involve sharing technical information with a general audience when that information affects the audience.
>
> - Debates in the personal and technical spheres engage a limited audience.
>
> - Public sphere debates engage a much larger audience than the other spheres and involve ordinary citizens and government officials. This sphere is the most important of the three because it is an essential activity for a democratic society.

3. Lead a discussion on the role of debate in democracy using some of the examples and ideas in Debate and Democracy: A Class Discussion. *(7 minutes)*

DEBATE AND DEMOCRACY: A CLASS DISCUSSION

Debate is essential to democracy. Consider the following types of dialogue and debate that occur daily in a public forum:

- Citizens in European countries arguing for and against the European Union Constitution

- American presidential candidates debating their stance on key voter issues

- Parliament debating the pros and cons of a proposed new law

- Pro-life supporters and scientists debating the use of stem cells in medicine

- A defense attorney and a prosecutor presenting evidence and arguments to support their cases to a judge or jury

- Disgruntled workers threatening to strike

- Students protesting a ban on head scarves

Ideas for Class Discussion:

1. Have your students discuss how each of these debate forums furthers democracy.

2. Have participants brainstorm other examples of dialogue or debate that further democracy. Ask them to justify their examples.

4. Discuss how the four key concepts—audience, evidence, reason, and language—function in public debate. *(7 minutes)*

KEY POINTS

- The audience for public debate is a general, not a technical, one, and debaters achieve excellence in public debate by addressing a universal audience.

- In the public sphere, arguments begin with the audience's knowledge but do not end there. Debaters offer new information and perspectives that add to the audience's knowledge.

- Reason is essential because it connects the evidence to the claim. Public debate uses a variety of argument forms, including informal logic, narrative, analogy, metaphor, etc.

- Language is the medium whereby the argument is presented. Consequently, the public debater must speak a language that a general audience can understand and find natural. Jargon distances the debater from the audience.

5. Teach Activity #10: "Audience Analysis" (*DTW* p. 214). *(15–20 minutes)*

6. Briefly explain how Karl Popper debate is a form of public argument. *(7–10 minutes)*

KEY POINTS

- Public debate can frequently degenerate into demagoguery, with speakers appealing to misconceptions and prejudice or using "sound bites" rather than extended, well-developed arguments to support their claims. In contrast, Karl Popper debate seeks to emulate the best of public debate.

- Judges in Karl Popper debate act as if they are well-informed members of the community. They evaluate debaters not on the technical dimension of argumentation and debate but on whether the debaters have designed their arguments to appeal to a universal audience and supported their claims with sound evidence and logic.

7. Break *(10 minutes)*

THE DEBATE CLUB IN THE SCHOOL COMMUNITY (TCO Y)

1. Teach Activity #42: "Team Mission Statement" (*DTW* p. 234). Arrange the students in groups and ask them to complete the activity. Make sure that all students are participating in their groups. Ask each group to present its mission statement to the class. Discuss the importance of teamwork and how completing this activity can help a debate team. *(20 minutes)*

2. Discuss the benefits of debate as an educational activity. *(3–5 minutes)*

> **KEY POINTS**
>
> - Debate develops critical thinking skills.
> - Debate fosters oratorical, public speaking skills.

3. Discuss the importance of fostering a spirit of inclusion and cooperation in a debate club. *(5 minutes)*

> **KEY POINTS**
>
> - Emphasize that the debaters should not think of themselves as individuals but as members of a team. They should view the team as a corporate entity working together to achieve a goal.
> - Fostering a spirit of inclusion and cooperation is vital for winning debates.
> - A team can create a sense of group identity through concrete steps: managing space, managing time, and developing club leadership and organization.

4. Teach Activity #43: "Team Constitution" (*DTW* p. 235). Ask the participants to work in their original groups and present a summary of their constitutions to the class. Discuss any difficulties the groups may have had and how completing this activity would benefit a debate team. *(20 minutes)*

5. Discuss the requirements for developing a collegial atmosphere in a debate club. *(10–15 minutes)*

KEY POINTS

- The club should have a room devoted to its activities. The room should have appropriate resources—reference materials, dictionaries, etc.—and space for club records.

- Clubs should meet regularly—one model suggests a mandatory meeting per week. Separate working sessions should be held for the team to construct arguments and strategies and, most important, to practice debating.

- While an adult will probably organize and lead the club, responsibilities should devolve to club members after the club is firmly established. Responsibilities should be shared by as many debate club members as are interested, and older members should train younger ones to make the club self-perpetuating.

- Educating students about debate—through holding discussions and presenting sample debates—is the most important step in recruiting.

6. Discuss the role of coaches, teachers, and parents in a debate club. *(10 minutes)*

KEY POINTS

- Coaches provide moral leadership for the team and foster the development of thinking skills by guiding the debaters rather than merely providing them with knowledge.

- Coaches handle the administrative work associated with the team: its schedule, roster, and finances.

- Parents can serve as judges or help with the logistics of tournaments. They also serve as sources of moral support for team members.

Wrap-up

Briefly review this week's objectives and TCOs and relate the activities and discussions from this class to each. Answer any remaining questions. *(3 minutes)*

ADDITIONAL ACTIVITIES

Chapter 17:
    Activity 3: "Debate Reporter" (*DTW* p. 210)
    Activity 5: "Student Parliament" (*DTW* p. 211)
    Activity 44: "Team Talk-a-thon" (*DTW* p. 236)

Week 2

OBJECTIVES

Students will be able to do the following:

1. Understand that the important elements of argument include claims, evidence, warrants, and reservations

2. Observe and create models to include claims, evidence, and warrants

3. Understand the difference between various argument structures, including simple arguments, convergent arguments, and independent arguments

4. Understand the purpose of and difference between claims and propositions

5. Understand the difference between the four categories of claims and propositions: definition, description, relationship, and evaluation

6. Understand that values are central to all four types of claims

CHAPTER FOCUS

DTW chapters 2 and 3

LESSON

WARM-UP

Explain to the students that they already have many of the skills relevant to debate, and teach Activity 1: "Skills Inventory" (*DTW* p. 209). (*5 minutes*)

THE STRUCTURE OF ARGUMENT (TCOs B & C)

1. Discuss the four basic elements of argument: claim, evidence, warrant, and reservation. Construct a simple Toulmin Model on the board with the four elements labeled. Explain how each element is crucial to the structure of an argument and use examples to illustrate each element. Note: The Toulmin Model is helpful in explaining the concept of argument, but it should NOT be used to construct a debate. (*10 minutes*)

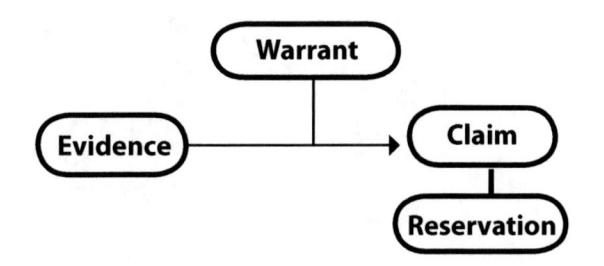

```
        Warrant
           |
Evidence ──┼──▶ Claim
              Reservation
```

> **KEY POINTS**
>
> - Warrant = reasoning process
> - Evidence = facts
> - Claim = controversial statement a debater intends to support using reasoned argument
> - Reservation = "but . . ." statement

2. Discuss the three structural types of argument—simple, convergent, and independent—and draw Toulmin models on the board for each type. *(15 minutes)*

> **KEY POINTS**
>
> - A simple argument contains a single claim leading from a single piece of evidence following a single warrant and may be accompanied by a single reservation. Your original diagram illustrates this type of argument: 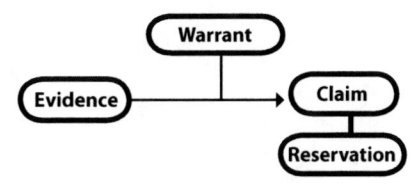
>
> ```
>           Warrant
>              |
>   Evidence ──┼──▶ Claim
>                 Reservation
> ```
>
> - A convergent argument contains two or more pieces of evidence to support a claim. Each piece of evidence is NOT enough to support the claim; the pieces support each other and thus the claim. The reservation may or not be present in the convergent argument.

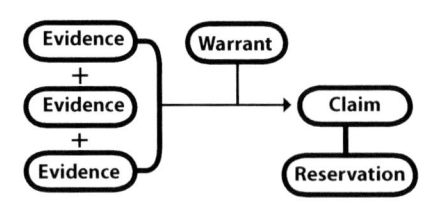

- An independent argument presents several pieces of evidence, any one of which provides sufficient support for the claim. Because each piece of evidence is sufficient, each has its own warrant to reach the claim.

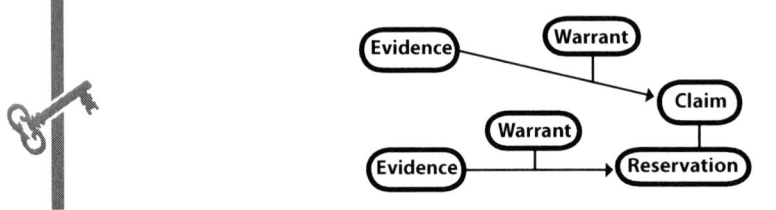

3. Ask the class for examples of arguments (or use those from the text) and write these on the board. Ask the class to determine structural type each is. Tell the class that they must justify their decision based on the evidence, warrants, and claim provided. *(5–10 minutes)*

4. Teach Activity 24: "Contention Creation Worksheet" (*DTW* p. 222). Ask the participants to convert ideas into structured claims. Be sure to ask the class to identify the type of argument structure used and draw the appropriate model to represent the argument. *(5–7 minutes)*

Claims and Propositions (TCO D)

1. Explain that claims and propositions are both controversial statements that a debater supports or refutes using evidence and warrants. Distinguish between claims and propositions. A claim is a narrower statement used to support a broader proposition. A proposition is the final claim the debater is making, and is usually supported by several claims, as shown in the following illustration. *(5–7 minutes)*

```
  Evidence  ─────▶  Claim  ┐
                            ├─────▶  Reservation
  Evidence  ─────▶  Claim  ┘
```

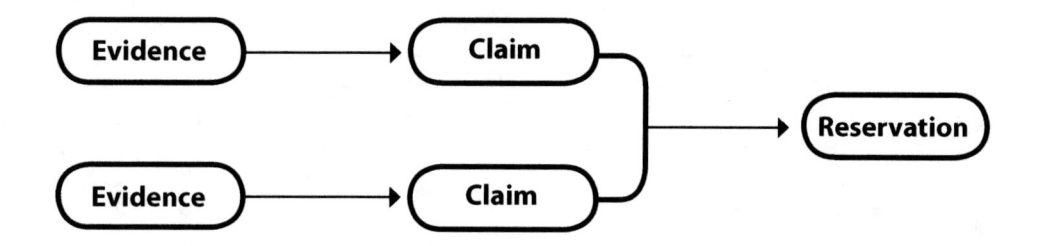

2. Distribute copies of the student worksheet Distinguishing between Claims, Propositions, and Evidence (p. 74). The sheet provides three blank Toulmin models. Tell the students that the second page of the worksheet contains statements that are evidence, claims, or propositions for three debate topics: censorship of the arts, affirmative action, and compulsory voting. Working alone, they are to write each statement in the correct blank on the appropriate model, so that they have three fully supported arguments. They are to use each statement only once. Give the students 5 to 10 minutes to complete the activity. *(15–20 minutes)*

3. Break *(10 minutes)*

4. Draw three blank Toulmin diagrams on the board using the following format:

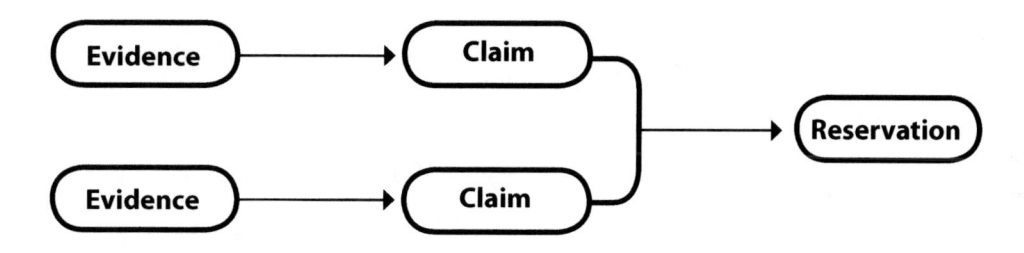

```
  Evidence  ─────▶  Claim  ┐
                            ├─────▶  Reservation
  Evidence  ─────▶  Claim  ┘
```

Label each diagram with one of the debate topics. Ask the class to consult their activity sheets to fill in the diagrams and justify the placement of each statement. Discuss each placement and help the students who placed their elements inappropriately. *(20 minutes)*

5. Explain the four types of claims and propositions. Refer the students to *DTW* p. 27 for a chart of the types with examples. *(20 minutes)*

KEY POINTS

- Propositions of definition—Assert that a certain definition ought to apply to a certain category of things.

- Propositions of description—Assert how people, institutions, processes, etc. should properly be described.

- Propositions of relationship—Assert something about how two or more objects, institutions, actions, etc. are related to one another. This type of proposition can be subdivided into two narrower categories: propositions of cause and effect and propositions of similarity.

  + Propositions of cause and effect assert that two or more people, objects, institutions, actions, etc. are related to each other via cause and effect.

  + Propositions of similarity assert that two or more people, objects, institutions, actions, etc. are similar to one another.

- Propositions of evaluation—These attach value judgments to objects, people, institutions, or ideas. These propositions can be subdivided into four categories: simple value propositions, comparative value propositions, simple policy propositions, and comparative policy propositions.

  + Simple value propositions attach some value to a person, object, institution, action, etc. without suggesting that a specific action be taken.

  + Comparative value propositions compare two or more persons, objects, institutions, actions, etc. without suggesting that a specific action should be taken.

  + Simple policy propositions urge some actor to take a specific action.

  + Comparative policy propositions suggest that some specific action is better than some other action.

6. Explain that understanding the differences between types of propositions can be confusing. Tell the students that they will play State the Proposition to help them distinguish the types. *(20 minutes)*

STATE THE PROPOSITION

Materials:

Sheet with the following propositions:

- Capital punishment deters would-be offenders. (Description)

- Capital punishment is unethical. (Simple value)

- Capital punishment is murder. (Similarity)

- Life imprisonment is more humane than execution. (Comparative value)

- All nations should abolish capital punishment. (Simple policy)

- A criminal is ANY person who breaks any law, whether by dropping litter or murdering another person. (Definition)

- Countries should focus more on trying accused murderers than on fighting for the rights of those already convicted. (Comparative policy)

- Capital punishment has increased the crime rate in many states. (Cause and effect)

Note: Focusing on one topic through several rounds allows the students to better see the difference between claims and propositions.

A. Have participants refer to the chart on *DTW* p. 27 for the definition of each type of proposition. Make sure that the students understand these definitions, and review if necessary.

B. Divide the class into four teams and tell them that they will be competing against each other in a game in which they will identify the types of propositions they have studied. Explain that they must identify the narrowest category. For example, if they think a statement is a proposition of relationship, they must determine whether it is a cause-and-effect proposition or a proposition of similarity. They must also explain their answer.

C. Ask the teams to select a spokesperson to report the team's answers. Once each team has selected its spokesperson, read a proposition aloud twice while the teams analyze it. The team whose spokesperson first raises his or her hand and correctly names the type AND justifies the team's decision scores one point.

(continued)

(continued)

    D. After you have received sufficient correct responses and you think that the students are ready, add random propositions that are not focused on one topic. Examples include the following:

- Freedom fighters are just terrorists. (Definition)

- Poverty is a disease. (Similarity)

- Americans, in particular, are responsible for global warming. (Cause and effect)

- Affirmative action is a good thing. (Simple value)

- Abortion is more humane than letting an unwanted child come into the world. (Comparative value)

- The World Health Organization needs to focus on eradicating HIV. (Simple policy)

Note: Some of the above can fall into more than one category. Consequently, it is important for the teams to justify their determination.

7. Discuss how values are central to all types of propositions. Analyze each type with the class and determine how each category deals with values, either implicitly or explicitly. *(15 minutes)*

8. Teach Activity 15: "Evaluate the Resolution" (*DTW* p. 217). After the students present their reasons for accepting or rejecting the resolutions, discuss what makes a good or bad resolution. *(20 minutes)*

Wrap-up

Briefly review this week's objectives and TCOs, and relate the activities and discussions from this class to each objective. Answer any remaining questions. *(3 minutes)*

Week 3

OBJECTIVES

Students will be able to do the following:

1. Differentiate between different types of evidence

2. Recognize when facts, theories, presumptions, values, and value hierarchies are used as evidence and know when to use them in an argument

3. Recognize evidence and use it in an argument

4. Construct Toulmin diagrams representing arguments with various types of warrants

5. Understand the necessity of a warrant and how to construct an argument using different types of warrants

6. Recognize and construct arguments using seven types of argumentative warrants: arguments by example, arguments by analogy, arguments of causality, arguments by authority, arguments of principle, arguments by incompatibility, and arguments by disassociation

CHAPTER FOCUS

DTW chapters 4 and 5

LESSON

Warm-up

Teach Activity 7: "Argument, Evidence and Explanation" (*DTW* p. 212). Compile a list of quotations and make sure that you have a quotation for each student. Instruct students to present their argument and quotation to a partner sitting next to them. That person should decide if the argument is relevant to the quotation. *(5 minutes)*

Types of Evidence (TCOs E and F)

1. Discuss the importance of evidence and describe the various categories into which evidence can be divided. *(60–70 minutes)*

KEY POINTS

- Evidence is the starting point of arguments.

- Evidence falls into two broad categories: that related to reality and that related to preference.

- Facts are individual pieces of data that either the debater or a third party has observed. Types of facts include these:

  + Examples and illustrations are factual data used to make specific statements about more general topics. Debaters can use a series of examples to prove a general rule, and employ an illustration to elucidate or clarify it. The persuasiveness of the argument depends in part on the number of examples the debater can produce and whether they are representative.

  + Historical descriptions are used as factual evidence when debaters need to present certain perspectives on past events or to use facts about historical events to support their arguments.

  + Statistics and parameters are commonly used to show what the public or a particular set of people thinks about a situation, or to highlight behavior. Statistics present the behavior or thinking of the whole based on a representative sample. Parameters provide total numbers, and so are better than statistics. However, they are often difficult or impossible to obtain.

  + Descriptions of empirical studies are sometimes more persuasive than "raw statistics" because they are based on underlying theoretical explanations as well as on figures.

  + Theories offer explanations or predictions—they are statements that have explanatory or predictive power.

- Presumptions do not depict reality but describe how people think reality is or ought to be. They are not always reliable, but they can be used to build on what the audience thinks it already knows as fact.

- Values are statements that provide evaluations of objects, persons, ideas, institutions, etc. Although we usually conceive of evidence as factual, values can be important sources of evidence, especially in claims of evaluation.

- Value hierarchies are statements that order values. They become important only when two values collide. In this situation, the debater uses value hierarchies to show that her value is more highly regarded.

2. Explain that one of a debater's most important tasks is evaluating evidence. Tell class members that they will be evaluating three types: statistics, theories, and presumptions.

   A. **Statistics:** Highlight how easily statistics can be skewed to prove a certain point. Give an example of how using a sample of 10 people for a population of 100, a pollster could ask how many of the 10 like Brad Pitt. If all 10 say they do not like Brad Pitt, the pollster could say that in polling a "representative sample" of the population, 0% likes Brad Pitt. However, in polling a different 10 from the same population, the pollster could find 100% likes Brad Pitt. Neither sampling used a representative group. Statistical samples are not always reliable, but they do carry a lot of weight as evidence in debates. Demonstrate this lack of reliability by conducting a mini-poll in the class. Count how many people are in the class. Using 10% of this number, ask them privately to state whether they prefer the color red or blue. Tally the results. Ask a different 10% of the class the same question privately and tally the results. Compare the results and see how they differ. Using a parameter, ask every student to vote for his or her favorite color—blue or red—and compare the finding with the statistical results.

   B. **Fact vs. Theory:** Tell the participants that they will be discussing the issue of Third World debt. Some of the **facts** are that debt was created 30+ years ago when interest rates were low and loans were liberally extended to developing countries. A number of factors came into play after the loans were extended: donor nations raised their interest rates; a number of the leaders of recipient nations embezzled significant amounts of the money; and they were often ousted in coups, leaving the countries with the debt and no feasible way to pay it back. The annual interest alone is prohibitive to many of these countries. They continue to sink further into poverty, with no monies left to educate, feed, and care for their citizens. One **theory** suggests that completely abolishing Third World debt will only encourage further corruption. The thinking is that if the lender nations forgive the debt, corrupt leaders have no incentive NOT to embezzle funds. Discuss the difference between facts and theory in this example and ask the students for their views on abolishment of debt. Make sure they explain their positions.

   C. **Presumptions:**

   - Quickly prompt the participants for the first thought that comes to mind when you say the following terms:
     Right-wing American
     Sunni Muslim
     White South African

   - Ask the students to share their thoughts with the class. What different presumptions did they have? Why did they think the way they did? Do people with similar backgrounds have the same or different presumptions?

3. Break *(10 minutes)*

ENRICHMENT SUGGESTIONS

- Ask the students to consider what debate resources are available where they live. Encourage students to watch/read the news from a variety of sources and compare the information gathered from each.

- Clip a page from a weekly news magazine or paper and analyze the material for biases, facts, examples, and illustrations.

- Stress the importance of reading as many viewpoints on an issue as possible, analyzing the evidence and warrants supporting the claims.

Warrants (TCOs G & H)

1. Discuss how warrants, while not always explicitly stated, are the means to reach the claim from the evidence. Give examples of how a warrant is developed within an argument. Although numerous types of warrants exist, this class will focus on seven of the most common types: arguments by example, by analogy, of causality, by authority, of principle, by incompatibility, and by disassociation. *(5 minutes)*

2. Define arguments by example (arguments that create an association between particular examples and a more general rule). Use the diagram from the textbook to illustrate the concept.

Evidence
Chomsky is un-American.

\+

Evidence
Rego is un-American.

\+

Evidence
Gilmore is un-American.

\+

Evidence
Qumsiyeh is un-American.

\+

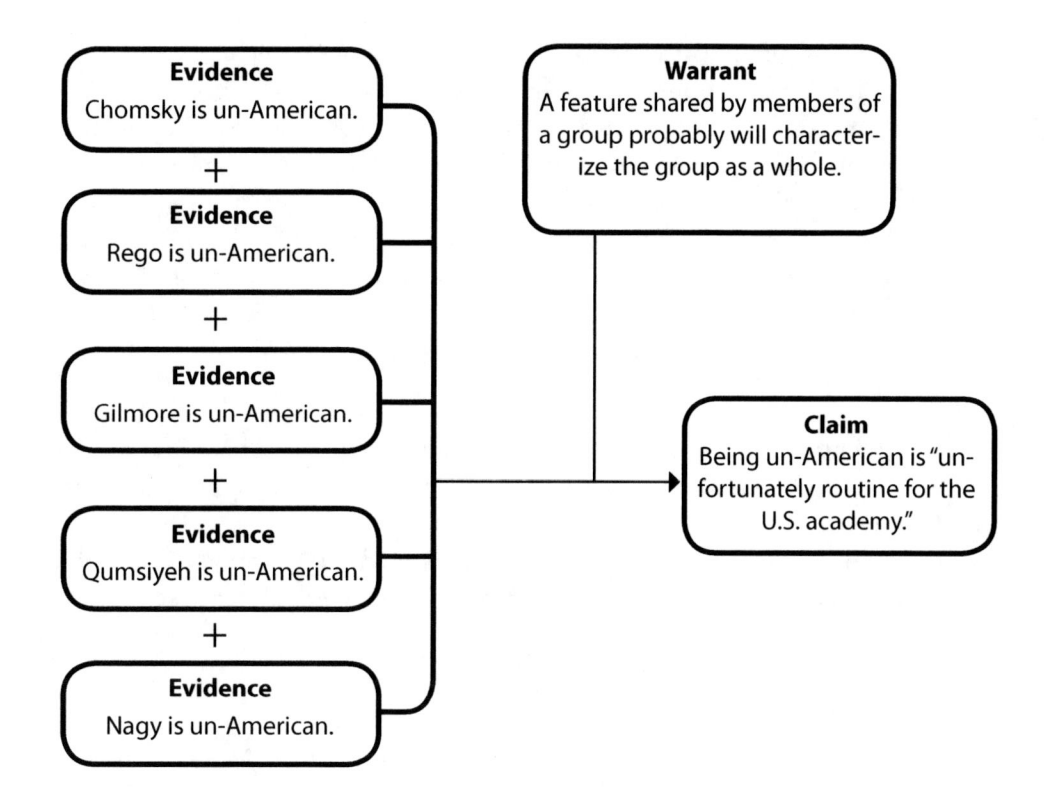

Evidence
Nagy is un-American.

Warrant
A feature shared by members of a group probably will characterize the group as a whole.

Claim
Being un-American is "unfortunately routine for the U.S. academy."

Draw the outline of the diagram in the textbook on the board, but leave out the actual evidence, warrant, and claim. Use the diagram to illustrate another argument by example, such as "male heads of government are eager to send their troops to war."

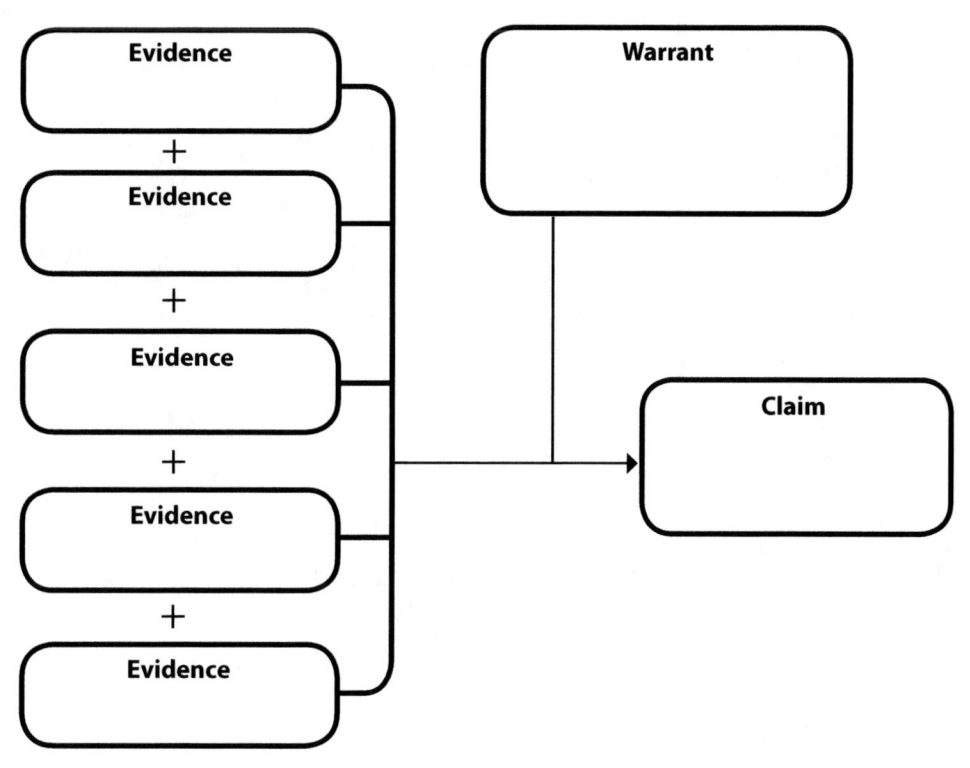

Evidence

\+

Evidence

\+

Evidence

\+

Evidence

\+

Evidence

Warrant

Claim

Write this claim in the claim box. Then insert an example of when a male leader readily sent troops into war in each of the evidence boxes. You will then have a diagram to support the claim. Note, however, that the students may come up with many examples of male leaders who do not send their troops into war. Tell the students that they have pointed to a weakness in this type of argument. The audience will accept the claim only if it accepts the warrant that the feature of the group characterizes the group as a whole. In this example, the students have offered evidence that challenges the argument. If there is time, have participants repeat the exercise using another claim. *(10 minutes)*

3. Arguments by analogy are similar to arguments by example in that two or more pieces of evidence are associated with each other to support a claim. However, arguments by analogy are based on an association of similarity rather than on a generalization. A claim is made about one member of a group based on the characteristics of other members. Three assumptions are made in arguments of analogy:

   ● Important similarities exist between the two cases.

   ● These similarities are relevant to the claimed relationship between the two cases.

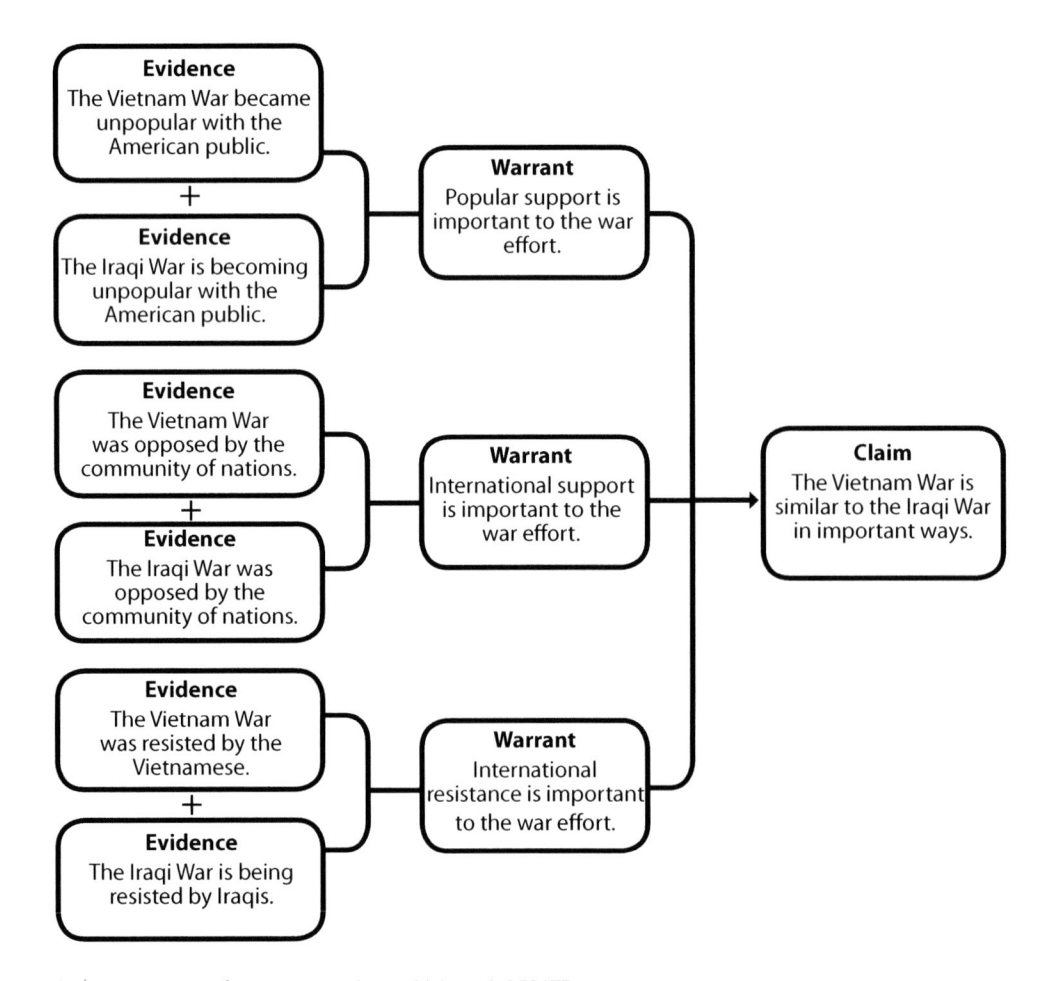

Evidence: The Vietnam War became unpopular with the American public.
+
Evidence: The Iraqi War is becoming unpopular with the American public.
→ **Warrant**: Popular support is important to the war effort.

Evidence: The Vietnam War was opposed by the community of nations.
+
Evidence: The Iraqi War was opposed by the community of nations.
→ **Warrant**: International support is important to the war effort.

Evidence: The Vietnam War was resisted by the Vietnamese.
+
Evidence: The Iraqi War is being resisted by Iraqis.
→ **Warrant**: International resistance is important to the war effort.

→ **Claim**: The Vietnam War is similar to the Iraqi War in important ways.

- Any differences between the two cases are not important to the claimed relationship.

Use the diagram from the textbook to illustrate this warrant. Ask the class to examine each piece of evidence, the warrants, and the claim and explain how the argument meets the three assumptions of argument by analogy. *(10–12 minutes)*

4. Arguments by causality (causal warrants) are used to construct arguments of cause and effect. They are difficult to create because we can only infer causes, not observe them. While evidence may suggest that one action causes another, it is difficult to prove causality conclusively. Ask the students to turn to the example in the textbook (p. 51), or copy the example on the board.

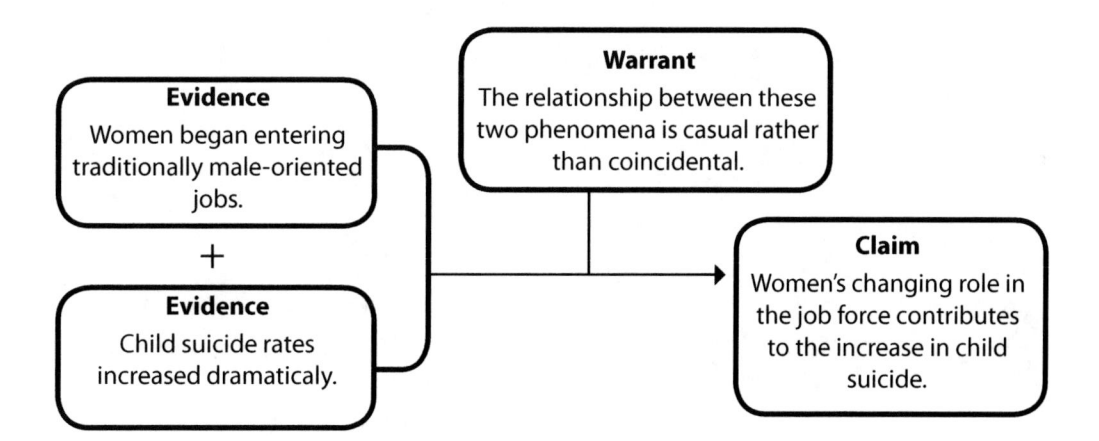

Evidence
Women began entering traditionally male-oriented jobs.

+

Evidence
Child suicide rates increased dramatically.

Warrant
The relationship between these two phenomena is casual rather than coincidental.

Claim
Women's changing role in the job force contributes to the increase in child suicide.

Lead a discussion of how strong the argument illustrated is and whether the stated effects are coincidental or causal. Then ask the students to build and diagram their own argument by causality. *(10 minutes)*

5. Arguments by authority are based on relationships between people and their actions. People may obtain authority from advanced degrees or sufficient experience in a field. This type of warrant can work in two ways: the arguer can be the actual authority OR she can quote those who are. Ask the class to turn to the example in the textbook (p. 53) or copy the example on the board.

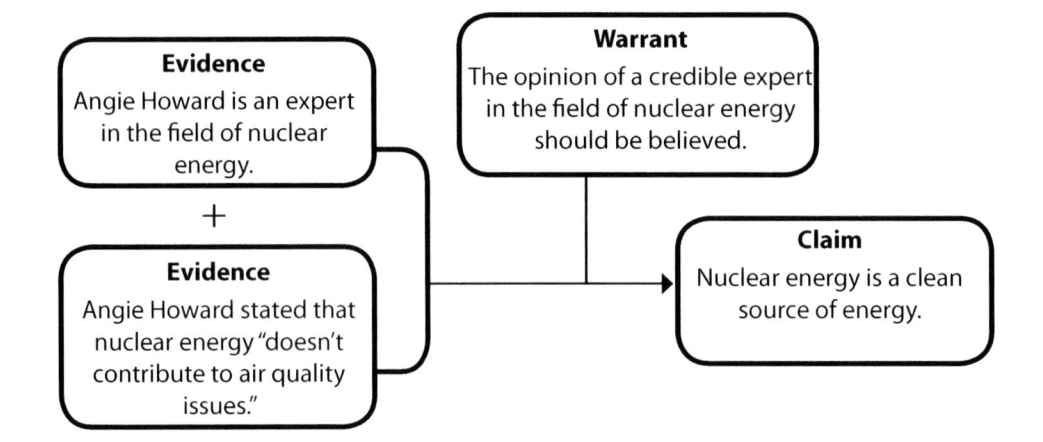

```
┌─────────────────────────┐      ┌──────────────────────────┐
│        Evidence         │      │         Warrant          │
│ Angie Howard is an expert│      │ The opinion of a credible expert │
│  in the field of nuclear │      │  in the field of nuclear energy  │
│         energy.         │      │     should be believed.          │
└─────────────────────────┘      └──────────────────────────┘
            +                                  │
┌─────────────────────────┐                    │
│        Evidence         │                    ▼
│  Angie Howard stated that│─────────▶┌──────────────────────┐
│ nuclear energy "doesn't │          │        Claim         │
│ contribute to air quality│          │ Nuclear energy is a clean│
│         issues."         │          │   source of energy.  │
└─────────────────────────┘          └──────────────────────┘
```

Discuss the example and then ask the students to develop and diagram their own argument by authority. *(10 minutes)*

If you wish the class to examine warrants of authority more deeply, you may use the accompanying lesson extension.

EXTENDING THE LESSON

The following lesson allows students with little technical information or authority to explore the importance of relevant, accurate, and complete evidence in arguments by authority. *(20 minutes)*

1. Read the following **bold** passages to your students. After each passage ask the short list of questions to ensure that the class understands the meaning of the passage.

    AIDS is the fourth leading cause of death worldwide. AIDS is the number one cause of death in Africa, and the majority of the world's deaths from AIDS occurs in Africa. The affected countries and AIDS health organizations do not have enough money to buy the drugs needed to treat all of Africa's AIDS and HIV patients.

    1. Is AIDS a health problem worldwide?

    2. What region of the world is hardest hit by the AIDS epidemic?

    3. Why can't people with HIV and AIDS take the medication they need?

    The HIV virus causes AIDS. Viruses must infect a cell to reproduce. HIV primarily infects cells in the immune system. Once the HIV virus binds to a cell, it hides its DNA inside the cell's DNA. When the cell reproduces, the virus reproduces as well. [1]

(continued)

(continued)

HIV significantly weakens or destroys the body's immune system, making the body susceptible to severe sickness and death from ailments such as a cold or pneumonia, which a normal body can easily fight off.

1. How does the HIV virus stay active and alive once it has infected a body?

2. What part of the body does the HIV virus primarily attack?

3. Can someone with AIDS die of a cold?

Nucleoside/Nucleotide Reverse Transcriptase Inhibitors (NRTIs) are one of the most effective types of drugs used in fighting HIV/AIDS. One of its makers, Manufacturer X, is willing to donate enough doses of NRTIs (but no additional drugs) to treat every HIV/AIDS victim in Africa for 10 years. NRTIs sell for $30 a pill in the United States, so this donation is very significant. No other drug maker is willing to make this kind of contribution, despite Manufacturer X's encouragement.

2. Write the following questions on the board and record the number of "yes" and "no" responses to each.

    1. Is Manufacturer X doing a good thing?

    2. Should AIDS activists protest the unwillingness of other drug makers to donate AIDS drugs?

    3. Should any restrictions be placed on Manufacturer X's donation?

    4. Should world health organizations have a say in whether Manufacturer X can give away this drug?

3. Now read the following text and ask the accompanying questions.

    NRTIs are a class of anti-HIV drugs. When NRTIs are used in combination with other anti-HIV drugs—usually a total of three drugs—this therapy can block the replication of HIV. NRTIs work by blocking the HIV virus from incorporating into the healthy genetic material of a cell, preventing the cell from producing more of the HIV virus.[2]

    1. Are NRTIs effective in blocking the reproduction of HIV in an infected body?

    2. Are NRTIs effective without any other anti-HIV drugs?

    NRTIs have some potential side effects, including fever, malaise, severe nausea, diarrhea, abdominal pain, sore throat, cough, shortness of breath, and rash.

(continued)

(continued)

They have also been associated with damage to the mitochondria (the cell parts that provide energy to the cell). These drugs may also cause muscle pain and wasting (particularly in the arms and legs), fatigue, damage to the nervous system, and, more rarely, serious liver or pancreas problems.[3] NRTIs keep HIV from reproducing in new cells but can damage or kill the white and red blood cells that the body needs to fight off infection. They may actually worsen an AIDS-infected person's health.

4. Refer back to the questions on the blackboard and ask them again based on this new information. Record the "yes" and "no" responses next to the previous tallies. These responses will differ from the earlier ones. Use this exercise to discuss the importance of researching a topic and determining what evidence to include when presenting an argument. In the example above, the initial evidence is faulty. Discuss

6. Arguments from principle involve justifying an action based on universal values. This type of argument usually has three parts:

   - A debater must select a principle.
   - The debater must argue for the importance of that principle.
   - The debater applies the action being contemplated to the principle.

   Ask the class to turn to the example on p. 56 of the textbook, or copy the example from the textbook onto the board

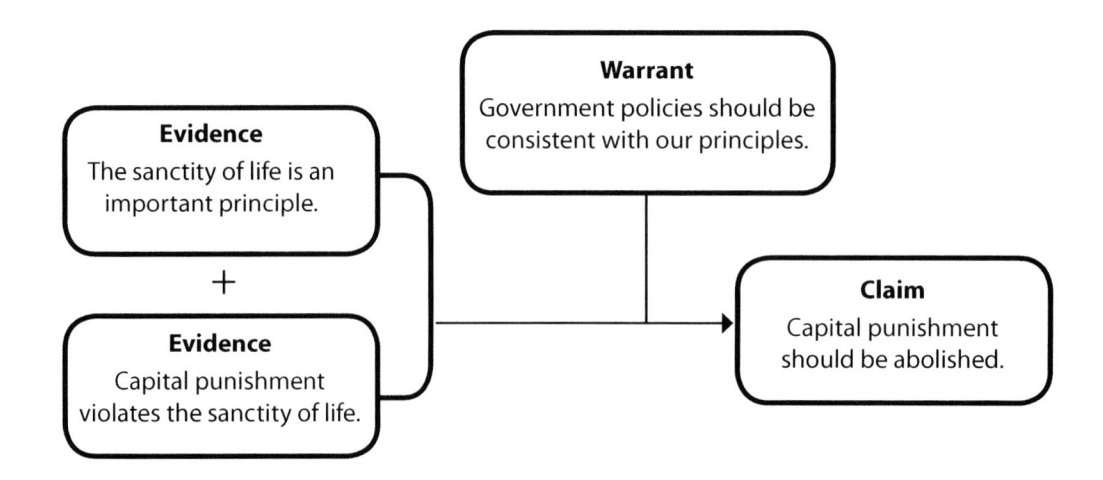

Evidence
The sanctity of life is an important principle.

+

Evidence
Capital punishment violates the sanctity of life.

Warrant
Government policies should be consistent with our principles.

Claim
Capital punishment should be abolished.

Ask the class to analyze the example and determine if it meets the three criteria. Then ask the students to develop and diagram their own example. Make sure that their argument has all three parts. *(10 minutes)*

7. Arguments by incompatibility are warrants intended to refute an opponent's argument and, by implication, support the debater's own. Questions to consider when analyzing whether an argument is one of incompatibility include the following:

    - Are the positions of the opposing debater accurately described?
    - Are the positions of the opposing debater based on the premises as described in the incompatibility argument?
    - Are the positions really incompatible?
    - Is the incompatibility significant?
    - To what extent does the argument by incompatibility support the debater's position?

    Ask the students to turn to the example in the textbook (p. 58) or copy the example on the board. Ask the students to explain how the argument answers the questions above.

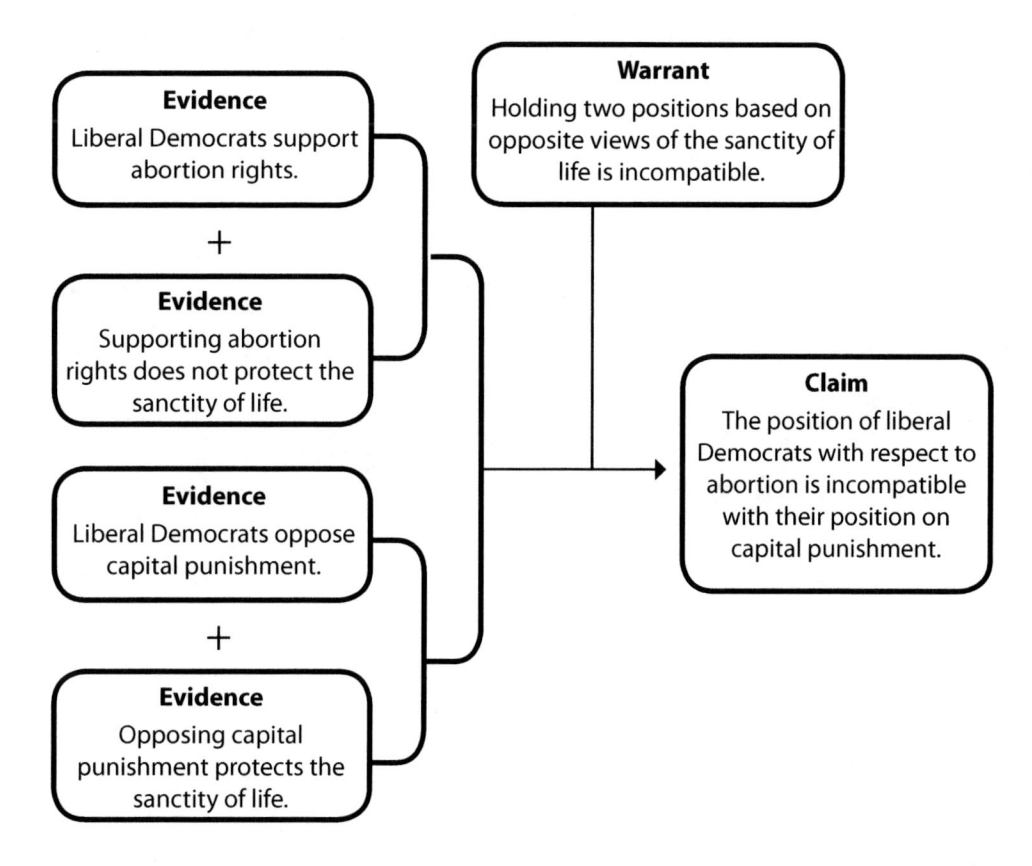

Evidence
Liberal Democrats support abortion rights.

+

Evidence
Supporting abortion rights does not protect the sanctity of life.

Evidence
Liberal Democrats oppose capital punishment.

+

Evidence
Opposing capital punishment protects the sanctity of life.

Warrant
Holding two positions based on opposite views of the sanctity of life is incompatible.

Claim
The position of liberal Democrats with respect to abortion is incompatible with their position on capital punishment.

Once the class has completed its analysis, ask them to develop and diagram another argument by incompatibility. Use the questions to help analyze the argument. *(10 minutes)*

8. Debaters use a disassociation warrant to counter an argument of incompatibility. This warrant divides (disassociates) a unified concept that the audience values into two different concepts—one that is valued and one that is not. After reviewing the example in the textbook (p. 60), ask the students to develop their own example. *(10 minutes)*

9. Teach Activity 45: "Argument Analysis" (*DTW* p. 237). *(10 minutes)*

Wrap-up

Briefly review this week's objectives and TCOs, and relate the activities and discussions from this class to each. Answer any remaining questions. *(3 minutes)*

Notes
1. http://www.aidsmeds.com/lessons/LifeCycleIntro.htm accessed May 5, 2006.
2. http://www.aidsmeds.com/NRTIs.htm#Question accessed May 5, 2006.
3. http://www.aidsmeds.com/lessons/DrugChart.htm accessed May 5, 2006.

Week 4

OBJECTIVES

Students will be able to do the following:

1. Identify the three criteria for logical assessment of an argument: acceptability, relevance, and sufficiency

2. Develop examples that meet the standards of acceptability, relevance, and/or sufficiency

3. Understand how fallacies violate the three criteria for logical assessment

4. Identify the three basic fallacies and common types within each category as well as fallacies related to language use

5. Understand the importance of acquiring both general and specific knowledge

6. Work as a team to develop a research plan

CHAPTER FOCUS

DTW chapters 6 and 12

LESSON

WARM-UP

Teach Activity 12: "Resolutional Analysis" (*DTW* p. 215). Allow participants time to discuss two topics they have come up with and observe them in pairs. *(5–7 minutes)*

THE QUALITY OF ARGUMENTS (TCOs I AND J)

Explain that in the previous weeks the class has focused on the components and structures involved in argumentation. The class will now focus on the logical criteria for determining what makes a good argument. A good argument must satisfy three criteria: acceptability, relevance, and sufficiency. *(20 minutes)*

KEY POINTS

- **The standard of acceptability** is related to evidence—the foundation of building a claim. No hard and fast rules exist for acceptability of evidence, but the text presents a table of general conditions for acceptability. If evidence meets one of these four conditions, it is acceptable enough to start an argument.

	Acceptability Conditions	
	Condition	Explanation
1.	Supported by a cogent subargument	Evidence is acceptable if the debater provides a cogent argument to support that evidence. In other words, evidence is acceptable to the extent that a debater provides good reasons for its acceptability.
2.	Common knowledge	Evidence may be considered "common knowledge" if it is known by virtually everyone in the debater's target audience.
3.	Supported elsewhere	A debater may note that the evidence is supported in some other source, usually a published source.
4.	Supported by a cogent subargument	A debater may use the opinion of an authority as evidence when that authority possesses specialized knowledge.

An example of each condition is listed below:

1. "The Palestinian people were rewarded for their hostile actions against Israel. This is obvious when Israel handed occupation of the Gaza Strip to the Palestinian people in 2005."

2. "There is no cure for AIDS"; or "Women are more often the victims of domestic abuse than are men."

3. A debater might cite evidence "proved" by a controlled study.

4. "According to the world-renowned advocate for children, UNICEF, one out of every three children in the world is living in poverty."

- **The standard of relevance** focuses on warrants—the reasoning that connects the evidence to the claim—and asks whether the connection is relevant. The following is an example of a warrant in which the evidence is not relevant to the claim:

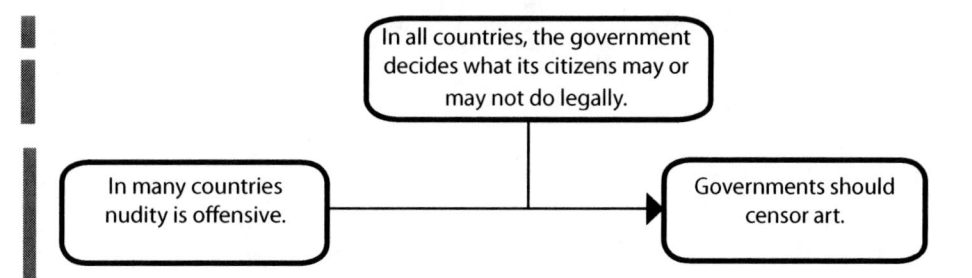

```
                    ┌─────────────────────────┐
                    │ In all countries, the    │
                    │ government decides what  │
                    │ its citizens may or      │
                    │ may not do legally.      │
                    └─────────────────────────┘

┌──────────────────┐                          ┌──────────────────┐
│ In many countries │ ──────────────────────→ │ Governments should│
│ nudity is offensive.│                       │ censor art.      │
└──────────────────┘                          └──────────────────┘
```

The warrant does not support the connection between the evidence and the claim because the evidence is not relevant to the claim.

Below is an example of a warrant in which the evidence is relevant to the claim:

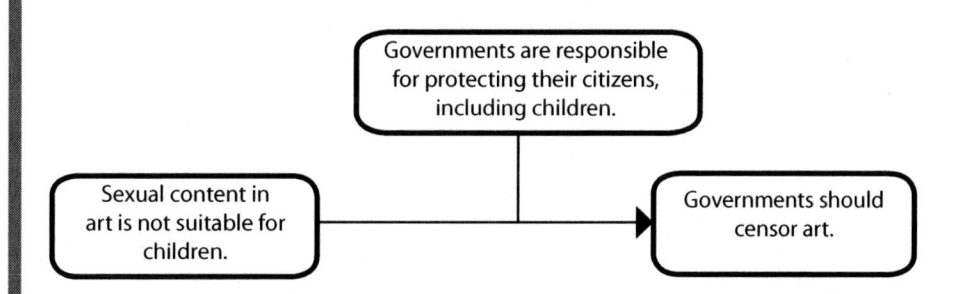

```
                    ┌─────────────────────────┐
                    │ Governments are responsible│
                    │ for protecting their citizens,│
                    │ including children.      │
                    └─────────────────────────┘

┌──────────────────┐                          ┌──────────────────┐
│ Sexual content in │ ──────────────────────→ │ Governments should│
│ art is not suitable for│                    │ censor art.      │
│ children.        │                          │                  │
└──────────────────┘                          └──────────────────┘
```

The warrant adequately supports the connection between the evidence and the claim.

- **The standard of sufficiency** involves how much certainty we require to accept the claim. This differs with context. For example, in the criminal justice system we demand proof beyond a reasonable doubt, while scientists require levels of significance over 95 percent.

Fallacies

1. Define "fallacy" (an error in reasoning that weakens or undermines the strength of an argument).

2. Discuss the three basic fallacies presented in the text—the problematic premise, the irrelevant reason, and the hasty conclusion—and point out that there is a fallacy for each of the three criteria for a logically adequate argument. Still other fallacies are related to language. They include the fallacy of ambiguity, the fallacy of equivocation, the fallacy of vagueness, and the fallacy of a loaded term. As you finish the discussion of each type,

ask the students for examples to ensure that they understand the concept. (*25 minutes*)

KEY POINTS

- **Problematic premises**—arguments that fail for any reason to fulfill the acceptability requirement. A premise is not problematic when it meets one of the four acceptability requirements mentioned above. Here are two variants of the problematic premise:

  + **Begging the question** occurs when a debater introduces a starting point or evidence that is the same as the claim. No argument exists because the evidence and claim are identical.

  + **The fallacy of incompatibility** occurs when a debater makes a statement as evidence that is at odds with another statement he made or when a debater's argument is incompatible with some action she has performed or recommended elsewhere.

- **Irrelevant reason**—arguments that fail to minimally satisfy the relevance criteria. Although clear-cut cases of irrelevancy are rare, three variants are common.

  + **An argument *ad hominem*** involves an attack on a person's character or background that is irrelevant to the claim.

  + **Straw person** fallacies involve arguments that sometimes intentionally misinterpret an opponent's argument. The debater then attacks the misconstrued argument, rather than the original.

  + **The red herring fallacy** shifts the focus from the current argument to one irrelevant to the discussion.

  Other fallacies of irrelevance discussed in the text include poisoning the well, guilt by association, appeal to fear, appeal to popularity, and appeal to tradition.

- **Hasty conclusions**—arguments that fail to meet the sufficiency criteria. While the argument may be relevant to the claim, the evidence is not sufficient to support it. The three most common types of hasty conclusions are these:

  + **Hasty generalizations** occur when the evidence is insufficient in number or is not representative of the whole.

- **Slippery slope** arguments are those in which a debater tries to connect a series of events in a causal chain that ultimately culminates in catastrophe.

- **The two wrongs** fallacy occurs when a debater tries to convince the audience that because something wrong was accepted or condoned, then a similar thing, also wrong, should be accepted.

- Other common types of fallacies of sufficiency include improper appeal to practice, fallacy of composition, fallacy of division, post hoc, and faulty analogy.

3. Break *(15 minutes)*

4. Teach Activity 46: "Name the Argument" *(DTW* p. 238). *(15 minutes)*

DEVELOPING RESEARCH SKILLS (TCO R)

1. Discuss the importance of research in helping a debater to become competent in arguing almost any topic. Emphasize that the research process involves two phases: gathering general knowledge and then gathering specific knowledge. *(15 minutes)*

   KEY POINTS

   - The two phases of research are the following:
     Phase 1: General Knowledge Research
       Stage 1: Locate background information
       Stage 2: Accumulate general knowledge
       Stage 3: Determine the vital, specific issues
       Stage 4: Review footnotes and bibliographies from the general sources to help find specific issues

     Phase 2: Specific Knowledge Research
       Stage 1: Outline the vital, specific issues
       Stage 2: Brainstorm concepts and key words relating to the specific issues
       Stage 3: Accumulate research on specific issues
       Stage 4: Review and research footnotes and bibliographies from the sources of general and specific knowledge

2. Discuss the various stages in Phase 1 for gathering general knowledge. When examining Stage 3, highlight the key questions involved in the stasis approach:

   - Question of existence

- Question of definition
- Question of quality
- Question of jurisdiction
- Question of cause

3. Ask the class to choose a debate topic or use one you have selected. Have the students develop specific questions to help focus the topic and gather general knowledge.

4. Explain that in Phase 2, debaters gather more specific knowledge after they better understand the general issues surrounding their topic. Ask the students to develop a plan for researching specific knowledge on their topic.

5. Teach Activity 19: "Source Selection" (*DTW* p. 219). *(10 minutes)*

6. For the remainder of the class session, gather the students in a library. Ask a librarian to provide a quick tour of the facility and make a brief presentation of the collection. Then conduct Library Research Activity. *(75 minutes)*

LIBRARY RESEARCH ACTIVITY

1. Divide the class into groups of four to five, and give each a general topic to research. Tell the groups that they have 3 minutes to determine if anyone in the group has existing knowledge of the topic. Once you call, "Time," they will have 15 minutes to use the resources available to gather general information on their topics. Remind them to note the sources they used so that they can review the footnotes and bibliographies later. They may assign specific areas within their topic to individual members of the group or work together to find the information. At the end of 15 minutes they will have an additional 5 minutes to share information among the members of their group.

2. Once the students have shared their information, help the groups organize their research so that they have an overview of what they have gathered.

3. Direct the groups to the stasis approach questions:
   - Question of existence

- Question of definition
- Question of quality
- Question of jurisdiction
- Question of cause

Instruct the groups to formulate questions about their topic using the information that they have been able to gather. Give the groups five minutes to generate their questions.

4. Now that the groups have developed their key questions, tell them to review the footnotes and bibliographies from their general sources. They have now completed Phase 1 of the General Knowledge Process. Prompt the class for any questions they may have about the process they just completed. Do they now have a better idea of the topic? Do they have an idea of what areas they need to develop in their search for specific knowledge?

5. Tell the groups that they will now gather specific knowledge. Remind them that their first step is to determine which questions they need to answer to gain a better grasp of the topics.

6. Tell the groups that they have 15 minutes to develop a list of specific questions they need answered on their topics.

7. Call, "Time" after 15 minutes. Tell the groups that they have 20 minutes to brainstorm concepts and fill in any gaps in their general knowledge and ensure that group members are aware of their next steps. They will then accumulate research on specific issues. They may work as they wish—each member gathering certain information or working as a group--to make sure that there are no gaps in their research. Ask if they have any questions and give them 20 minutes of research time.

8. Call, "Time" after 20 minutes. Tell the participants that they have the next 5 minutes to collate their research, review footnotes and bibliographies, remove redundant research, and ensure that other gaps in knowledge are filled.

Wrap-up

Briefly review this week's objectives and TCOs and relate the activities and discussions from this class to each. Answer any remaining questions. *(3 minutes)*

ADDITIONAL ACTIVITIES

Chapter 6:
- Activity 9: "'Real World' Debate" (*DTW* p. 213)
- Activity 16: "Selective Definition" (*DTW* p. 217)
- Activity 47: "Fallacy Fantasy Land" (*DTW* p. 239)

Chapter 12:
- Activity 17: "Dictionary Challenge" (*DTW* p. 218)
- Activity 18: "Guided Research" (*DTW* p. 218)

Week 5

OBJECTIVES

Students will be able to do the following:

1. Understand the sections and features of the Karl Popper debate format and recognize various sections in play

2. Work as a team to analyze an abbreviated version of a Karl Popper debate

CHAPTER FOCUS

DTW chapter 7

LESSON

Warm-up

Discuss how debate is essential to a dynamic democracy. Consider the following types of dialogue and debate that occur daily in public forums:

- European citizens in individual countries arguing for and against the EU Constitution
- American presidential candidates debating their stance on key issues
- Parliament debating the pros and cons of a proposed new law
- Pro-life supporters and scientists debating the use of stem cells in ailing patients
- A defendant and a prosecutor presenting evidence and arguments to support their case to a judge or jury
- Disgruntled workers threatening to strike
- Students protesting a ban on head scarves

1. Ask the students how each of these debate forums furthers democracy.

2. Have participants brainstorm other examples of dialogue or debate that further democracy. Ask them to justify their choices.

3. Discuss ways in which debate is used in a school setting. *(5 minutes)*

The Karl Popper Debate Format (TCO K & U)

1. Tell the class that this week's lesson will focus on the Karl Popper debate format. Explain that this format can be used to debate any kind of proposition. Karl Popper debates aim to develop the following:

   - Critical thinking
   - Tolerance for different views
   - Education
   - Respect for general ethical principles
   - Humbleness when debating opponents
   - Creation of an informed democratic citizenry

   Discuss why these goals are important in dynamic democracies. *(10 minutes)*

2. Discuss each section of the Karl Popper debate format in detail, focusing on the purpose of each section, the debater's responsibilities, and the time restrictions. You may refer to the chart on p. 82 of the textbook or use the chart below. *(15 minutes)*

Karl Popper Debate Format Guidelines

	Section	Time	Speaker
1.	Affirmative Constructive	6 minutes	First Affirmative Speaker
2.	Cross-Examination	3 minutes	Third Negative Speaker questions First Affirmative Speaker answers
3.	Negative Constructive	6 minutes	First Negative Speaker
4.	Cross-Examination	3 minutes	Third Affirmative Speaker questions First Negative Speaker answers
5.	First Affirmative Rebuttal	5 minutes	Second Affirmative Speaker
6.	Cross-Examination	3 minutes	First Negative Speaker questions Second Affirmative Speaker answers
7.	First Negative Rebuttal	5 minutes	Second Negative Speaker
8.	Cross-Examination	3 minutes	First Affirmative Speaker questions Second Negative Speaker answers
9.	Final Affirmative Rebuttal	5 minutes	Third Affirmative Speaker
10.	Final Negative Rebuttal	5 minutes	Third Negative Speaker

3. Discuss each section of the format in detail, focusing on the purpose of each section, the debater's responsibilities, and the time restrictions. Emphasize that the Karl Popper format requires debaters to work as a team and value the importance of the team concept. If debaters cannot work as a team, they and their team cannot succeed. *(15 minutes)*

4. Distribute copies of Karl Popper Quotes (p. 76). Organize the class into groups of three or four and ask the groups to discuss within their groups what each quote means and how Popper's words influenced the debate format that bears his name. *(10 minutes)*

5. Tell the students that while they will have the opportunity to watch or hear a debate, they will also learn the important skill of flowing. Explain that flowing is essentially an abbreviated version of a debate written on as little as one sheet of paper, but certainly more sheets can be used. Audience members may flow a debate they are observing, but more importantly, judges flow a debate to ensure that all arguments have been responded to appropriately and to help decide who won the debate. Describe the basics of flowing.

6. Use Activity #23, "Demonstration Debate" (*DTW* p. 221) to have the class practice flowing. You may use the debate transcript at the back of the text or use a video or audio version of another Karl Popper format debate. Provide participants with copies of the Argument Flow Sheet (p. 90). Depending on the debate format that will be presented to the students, have them divide their paper into an appropriate number of columns to allow one column for each speech throughout the duration of the debate. Reiterate basic flowing procedure. *(30–45 minutes)*

7. Break *(10 minutes)*

8. Discuss with the class their observations of the flow of the debate. Focus on how the team worked together to present their views and oppose the other team's.

9. Discuss the importance of preparation time and explain how debaters can use it strategically. *(5 minutes)*

10. Form the class into groups of two or three and distribute copies of Group Discussion Questions for Karl Popper Debate Transcript and Commentary Reading (p. 78) to the students. Ask them to silently read the sample debate transcript and the commentary in the text. After reading each section, they will work together in their groups to answer a brief list of questions. Alert them that at certain points in the activity each group member must provide his or her own response. *(60 minutes)*

11. Collect the worksheets and ask the class for their reactions to the activity. Do they feel more comfortable with the format? Can they see how the format's target goals came into play. *(5 minutes)*

Wrap-up

Briefly review this week's objectives and TCOs, and relate the activities and discussions from this class to each. Answer any remaining questions. *(3 minutes)*

ADDITIONAL ACTIVITIES

Chapter 7:
    Activity 2: "Debate of the Masses" (*DTW* p. 209)
    Activity 11: "Brainstorming" (*DTW* p. 215)
    Activity 22: "Impromptu Format Debate" (*DTW* p. 220)

Week 6

OBJECTIVES

Students will be able to do the following:

1. Identify the three parts of a causal argument

2. Identify and demonstrate three common methods used to support and refute cause-and-effect arguments

3. Name important types of causes of a resolution, including necessary and sufficient causes, contributory causes, and intervening or counteracting causes

4. Demonstrate the construction and refutation of a causal argument

CHAPTER FOCUS

DTW chapter 8

LESSON

WARM-UP

Teach Activity 14: "Name That Proposition" (*DTW* pp. 216–17), which reviews different types of propositions. *(7 minutes)*

CONSTRUCTING ARGUMENTS ABOUT CLAIMS OF CAUSE AND EFFECT (TCOs M & L)

1. Explain that during the next three weeks students will focus on constructing different kinds of argument. This week, the class will focus on constructing arguments using cause-and-effect relationships. The students will also learn how to debate against these types of arguments. *(3 minutes)*

2. Point out that cause-and-effect reasoning is common in everyday discussions. If your lights don't go on, you think that the electricity is out. Debaters use the same type of reasoning when arguing propositions. They make connections between causes and effects and work to establish the warrants between their evidence and the claims. *(5 minutes)*

3. Explain that a causal argument has three parts: the description of the cause, the description of an effect, and the demonstration of the causal

relationship between the two. Ask the class for examples of cause-and-effect relationships they encounter regularly. *(10 minutes)*

> **KEY POINTS**
>
> - Arguers frequently describe an alleged cause by observing a phenomenon.
> - They then describe the effect, often by pointing to another phenomenon.
> - After having described both the cause and effect, they then demonstrate that the relationship between the two described phenomena is causal.

4. Explain that because constructing arguments about cause and effect often relies on inferred, NOT observed, causes, debaters can use three methods to support and refute causal reasoning. These methods are method of agreement, method of difference, and method of correlation. *(20 minutes)*

> **KEY POINTS**
>
> - The method of agreement points to more than one case in which two elements are simultaneously present. Having presented these cases, the debater then claims that one element is the cause and the other is the effect. The method of agreement, especially when used alone, is particularly susceptible to error. Use the excellent example in the textbook (p. 90) to emphasize this point.
> - The method of difference requires examples in which both the suspected cause and the suspected effect are absent. Debaters can combine this method with the method of agreement to provide a stronger argument. Debaters can also use this method to uncover fallacies when an opponent uses the method of agreement.
> - The method of correlation can be used to demonstrate that as the amount of the cause increases or decreases, the effect will also increase or decrease. It can also serve as a check on a false cause-and-effect argument.

5. Break *(10 minutes)*

6. Tell the students that they will now construct and refute causal arguments. *(Total time for this activity depends on the size of the group, but typically 65–80 minutes)*

A. Organize the class into groups of four and distribute Arguing and Refuting Causal Relationships worksheet (p. 82).

B. Explain that each group is to use the paragraph to demonstrate the different methods for showing cause and effect between the evidence and the claim:

- method of argument
- method of difference
- method of correlation

They are also to demonstrate the three elements necessary in constructing a cause-and-effect argument:
1. describing features of the cause
2. demonstrating the effect
3. demonstrating a causal relationship

C. Once they have completed the task, groups will present their arguments to the class, which will analyze them.

(Allow 10 minutes for giving directions, assembling into groups, and getting the class started. Allow 15 minutes for the groups to work together and an additional 5–8 minutes for each group to present its arguments)

7. Define and illustrate the four types of causal arguments presented in the text: necessary, sufficient, contributory, and intervening. *(15 minutes)*

KEY POINTS

- Necessary causal arguments state that without the suspected cause, the effect cannot occur.
- Sufficient causal arguments argue that the presence of the effect virtually guarantees the cause.
- Contributory causal arguments recognize that the purported cause may be one of the many contributors to the effect.
- Intervening and counteracting causal arguments are those that prevent the completion of a cause-and-effect sequence.

8. From their completed Arguing and Refuting Causal Relationships worksheets, ask the students to call out examples of the four types of causal arguments. Write these on the board and label each for participants to take notes. *(10–15 minutes)*

9. Explain that to refute a cause-and-effect argument, a debater must critically examine other possible causes, the effects, and the relationship between the two. To refute this type of argument, debaters can refute the description of the cause, show alternative causes of the effect, disagree with the alleged effect, or demonstrate that the relationship is not causal. *(15 minutes)*

KEY POINTS

- Refuting the affirmative's description of the cause involves questioning the affirmative's description of the cause.

- Showing alternative causes of the effect is useful when the affirmative has used the method of agreement in its analysis because that method is highly susceptible to error.

- In cases when the negative agrees with the affirmative's identified cause, it may challenge the existence of the effect the affirmative has argued.

- Showing that the relationship is not causal is the most important option available to the negative.

- When preparing its case, the negative should keep in mind logical fallacies accompanying cause-and-effect reasoning.

Wrap-up

Briefly review this week's objectives and TCOs, and relate the activities and discussions from this class to each. Answer any remaining questions. *(3 minutes)*

Week 7

OBJECTIVES

Students will be able to do the following:

1. Differentiate between a cause-and-effect proposition and a value proposition
2. Differentiate between a simple value proposition and a comparative value proposition
3. Demonstrate how to support value propositions through combining descriptive, relational, and evaluative claims
4. Construct an argument to oppose a value proposition by building a coherent negative case

CHAPTER FOCUS

DTW chapter 9

LESSON

WARM-UP

Review the various ways to construct arguments about cause and effect. Tell the students that today's lesson will focus on constructing arguments about claims of value, and it is important to remember the difference between the various types of arguments. *(5 minutes)*

CONSTRUCTIVE ARGUMENTS ABOUT CLAIMS OF VALUE (TCOs L, N, & O)

1. Explain that this class session will focus on simple and comparative value claims and define each. Prompt the class for examples. *(10 minutes)*

   KEY POINTS

   - Simple value claims attach a value to an object (a person, place, thing, institution, action, concept, etc.).

   - Comparative value claims compare two or more objects with respect to some value—essentially arranging the objects in a hierarchy.

2. Explain how to support a simple value claim by combining three kinds of claims: descriptive, relational, and evaluative. (*20 minutes*)

KEY POINTS

- Debaters can support a simple value claim by

    1. Describing one or more features of the object of evaluation;

    2. Relating those features to some effect; and

    3. Evaluating those effects.

3. Distribute copies of Building a Case for and against a Simple Value Proposition worksheet (p. 83) to each student. Ask the students to read the passage, and based on what they have learned about constructing simple value propositions, complete the outline in Part 1. When everyone has finished, discuss the responses. (Remind the students that they will need their worksheets later in the lesson.) (*30 minutes*)

4. Explain that the class will now learn to construct an argument for a comparative value proposition. Emphasize that any comparison of two or more objects typically assumes there is some conflict in value between the objects and that the construction of the argument must keep this expectation in mind. Stress that the students must evaluate each of the arguments. (*25 minutes*)

KEY POINTS

- Supporting a comparative value proposition follows the same process—describe, relate, evaluate—as supporting a simple value proposition, but the process must be applied to each argument.

5. Distribute copies of Building a Case for a Comparative Value Proposition worksheet (p. 86) to each participant and divide the class into pairs. Explain that each pair is to work together to develop a comparative proposition of value based on the passage in the worksheet. Remind them that they must fill in the descriptive, relational, and evaluative claims for EACH argument as well as an overall conclusion. When everyone has finished, ask the pairs to provide their responses, and discuss them as a class. (*50 minutes*)

6. Explain that you will discuss three ways to oppose value propositions using constructive arguments, and give the students an opportunity to practice them. The three ways you will discuss are arguments with respect to description, arguments with respect to causal relationships, and arguments with respect to evaluation. As you discuss each, give examples and prompt the class for additional examples. *(30 minutes)*

KEY POINTS

- The negative can oppose **descriptive** arguments by
  + rejecting the features described by the affirmative (e.g., proving that the features the affirmative chose to highlight are incorrect);
  + describing other features ignored by the affirmative.

- The negative can oppose arguments with respect to **causal** relationships by
  + showing that the affirmative's features are not related to the effects suggested;
  + demonstrating that other effects are related to the features the affirmative did suggest;
  + demonstrating effects of features other than those the affirmative suggested.

- The negative can oppose **evaluative** arguments in many ways, including
  + associating other values with the affirmative effects;
  + arguing that the affirmative value is not important or that the negative's points hold more value than the affirmative's;
  + associating the affirmative's values with negative's effects.

7. Explain that the negative cannot merely respond point-by-point to affirmative's claims. To do so makes that team appear reactive rather than proactive. To win the debate, the negative must present the judge with a well-organized and coherent position that explains why they oppose the proposition. *(10 minutes)*

8. To ensure that participants understand how to construct an argument to oppose value propositions, refer them back to the Building a Case for and against a Simple Value Proposition worksheets they partially completed earlier in this session. Tell them to work alone to complete Part 2, building

a negative case based on the information they formulated for the affirmative. Remind the students to provide the descriptive, relational, and evaluative claims for EACH argument provided, and offer an independent argument to support the negative's view. Give the students 10 minutes to complete the assignment. When everyone has finished, lead a class discussion based on the students' responses. *(20 minutes)*

WRAP-UP

Briefly review this week's objectives and TCOs, and relate the activities and discussions from this class to each. Answer any remaining questions. *(3 minutes)*

Week 8

OBJECTIVES

Students will be able to do the following:

1. Understand the difference between a simple policy proposition and a comparative policy proposition
2. Understand the roles of the affirmative and negative in presenting each
3. Construct a need-plan-benefits case
4. Understand the options in arguing a policy proposition

CHAPTER FOCUS

DTW chapter 10

LESSON

Warm-up

Note: Because this chapter and class session are incredibly content-rich, we recommend that you begin the class by writing an outline of the major points from the chapter (*DTW* p. 133) on the board. We have included a minimum of structured activities in this session because we suggest that you teach to each point, using examples to clarify the key concepts. When possible, prompt the students for the examples and try to maintain those examples as you teach each step. Of course, you can always use a structured activity if you wish, but this week's content seeks to clarify the material offered in the text.

As a Warm-up, review the various types of claims, and explain the format of this week's session. *(10 minutes)*

Arguing about Simple Policy Propositions (TCOs L & P)

1. Explain that policy claims explicitly call for some kind of action, such as abolishing a law or changing policy on a social issue.

2. Describe the two different kinds of policy propositions: simple policy propositions and comparative policy propositions. Using examples of policy propositions that appeal to your students, discuss how simple and comparative policy propositions would differ in each instance. *(20 minutes)*

KEY POINTS

- In simple policy propositions, the affirmative supports a change in the status quo, while the negative typically defends the current policy.

- In comparative policy propositions, each team defends a different change in policy. The affirmative does not typically defend the status quo.

3. Discuss the role that values play in policy claims and prompt the students for examples of claims in which value and policy are strongly intertwined. (*10 minutes*)

4. Explain how to use the need-plan-benefit strategy to construct a simple policy case. (Remind the students that only the affirmative proposes this strategy.) List the steps in developing this strategy on the board as you review each in detail. Ask the class for an example of a policy proposition that you can use to illustrate each point as you present it. (*20 minutes*)

KEY POINTS

- Identify some **need** caused by the present situation.

    + Identify a problem in the current policy or status quo and correlate it to a commonly held value.

    + Identify the cause of the problem that the plan will solve.

    + Demonstrate that the present system cannot solve the problem because of gaps or inconsistencies in the current policy.

- Propose a **plan** to solve the problem. Typically, the plan contains both essential and nonessential elements.

    + Essential elements include an action—the proposed change in policy—and an actor who will carry out the plan (the WHAT and WHO of the plan).

    + Nonessential elements include the details of the plan's implementation (the HOW, WHERE, and WHEN of the plan).

- Demonstrate the **benefits** of the new plan. Show how the proposed strategy solves or reduces the problem.

5. Discuss how the negative can attack a need-plan-benefit strategy. Explain that the negative team usually has the advantage because they are defending an existing policy, which enjoys the privilege of presumption. Change requires effort and risk, and so the affirmative must convince the people that the benefits of change outweigh the risks of maintaining the status quo. In defending the concept of presumption, the negative can use three specific strategies: defending the status quo, defending a policy other than the status quo, and attacking the plan. *(20 minutes)*

KEY POINTS

- In **defending the status quo** the negative has three options:
    + Argue that the problem does not exist or is not very serious.
    + Argue that the present system can solve the problem.
    + Argue that the affirmative has identified the wrong cause.

- The negative can consider **defending a plan other than the status quo.** The negative can choose this strategy when the current policy has more problems that the negative wishes to defend, or when the negative has a superior alternative to the status quo AND to the affirmative's plan. The negative has two options:
    + Advocate minor repairs to the present system.
    + Present a counterplan. In this case the negative must propose a counterplan that conforms to all the requirements of an affirmative plan (presented earlier in the class session) and is an alternative, not an addition, to the affirmative plan.

- **Attack the plan.** They can argue that
    + the affirmative's plan will not work;
    + the affirmative's plan will not solve the problem because it has identified the wrong cause;
    + the affirmative's plan will cause disadvantages.

6. Break *(10 minutes)*

Constructing Arguments to Support a Claim of Comparative Policy

1. Answer any remaining questions the class may have about simple policy propositions. And explain that the class will now focus on constructing arguments of comparative policy claims. *(10 minutes)*

2. Remind the class that comparative policy propositions have stances assigned to both the affirmative and the negative teams and that the roles and responsibilities differ for each team. *(5 minutes)*

3. Explain that in this type of debate, the affirmative must compare a given policy not with the status quo but to a particular policy assigned to the negative by the same proposition. The most straightforward way to do this is to use a comparative advantage analysis. This analysis has three distinct phases: conceptualizing the case, creating the plan, and constructing the advantages. Explain the three steps in greater detail. *(25 minutes)*

KEY POINTS

- **Conceptualize the case** by asking a series of questions to assess and define the competing policies. Questions to consider include these:

    + What are the central features of both policy options?

    + How do features of these policy options interact with one another?

    + How can some feature of the affirmative plan be used to replace some feature of the negative policy?

    By answering these questions, debaters focus on the features of the negative policy they must avoid and the features of their plan they must highlight. Having thought about the proposition, the team can then begin building its case.

- **Creating the plan** by modifying an existing plan or making a new one. One significant difference between a simple and complex policy plan is that while a simple policy plan merely states a policy, the comparative policy plan must account for the interaction of the features of the affirmative and negative plans. The affirmative must do the following:

    + create a list of features of the negative policy it will exclude from its plan;

    + develop a more detailed list of categories and subcategories of these policies that it will exclude from its plan;

- + create a list of features it wants to include in its plan;
- + develop a detailed list of categories and subcategories of these policies that it will include in its plan.

- **Construct the advantages** by researching the comparative costs and benefits of both the affirmative and negative plans and determining which specific advantages of its plan to include in its case. For each advantage, the case should do the following:

  - + describe the feature of the negative plan that is meant to address the problem;
  - + describe the reasons why the negative strategy does not achieve the advantage;
  - + describe the feature of the affirmative plan that deals with problem;
  - + describe the reasons why the affirmative plan achieves the advantage.
  - + The affirmative could also construct advantages using the following four steps:
    1. describe an inherent feature of the policy associated with the negative policy;
    2. relate that condition to some unwanted effect;
    3. describe an opposing condition associated with the affirmative policy;
    4. relate that condition to some positive effect.

  To decide which method to follow, the affirmative should determine which approach provides the most advantages for it AND is least advantageous to the negative.

4. Explain that the negative uses the same steps to develop its case. *(10 minutes)*

5. Tell the students that they will now put their knowledge of constructing policy claims into practice.

   A. Arrange the class into groups of six and randomly assign three students in each group to be the negative team and three to be the affirmative. (The groups are to mimic those used in the Karl Popper format. If you cannot divide your class into groups of six, form as many even numbered groups as possible. Ideally you want at least two individuals in each affirmative and negative team.)

B. Explain that you will give each group a policy proposition. The group as a whole will have 10 minutes to work together to conceptualize the case, develop a plan, and construct the advantages that the affirmative will present and the disadvantages or counterplan that the negative will present. After 10 minutes, each team will present its plan or counterplan and its evaluation of the opponent's plan or counterplan and stance.

C. Make sure that all students understand and answer any questions about the activity.

D. Now, assign a policy proposition to each group. State whether it is a simple or comparative policy claim, and assign a stance to each team. Give each team 10 minutes to work as a group.

E. After 10 minutes, ask one group to come to the front. The affirmative team in the group will present its plan and advantages. The negative will then present the disadvantages and/or counterplan.

F. After the groups present, ask the rest of the class for a reaction to each group's presentations and for suggestions on a different angle or plan for either the affirmative or negative. After the class provides feedback, add any comments you have.

G. Repeat the procedure until all groups have finished.

Wrap-up

Briefly review this week's objectives and TCOs, and relate the activities and discussions from this class to each. Answer any remaining questions. (*3 minutes*)

Week 9

OBJECTIVES

Students will be able to do the following:

1. Understand the importance of refutation

2. Apply the five steps in refutation

3. Offer rebuttals by identifying key issues, summarizing vital points, making critical choices, and weighing the implications of their arguments

4. Understand the purposes and importance of cross-examination

5. Utilize effective questioning and responding techniques in cross-examination

CHAPTER FOCUS

DTW chapters 11 and 13

LESSON

WARM-UP

1. Review how to construct arguments for value, cause-and-effect, and policy propositions. Discuss why it is important to be able to differentiate between the types and understand how the affirmative and negative should debate each.

2. Explain that this session will focus on refutation, rebuttals, and cross-examination—the very reason that debates consist of more than just persuasive speeches by two different teams.

3. Finally, briefly review the format of Karl Popper debate and the responsibilities of each of the speakers. *(10–15 minutes)*

Karl Popper Debate Format Guidelines		
Section	Time	Speaker
1. Affirmative Constructive	6 minutes	First Affirmative Speaker
2. Cross-Examination	3 minutes	Third Negative Speaker questions First Affirmative Speaker answers
3. Negative Constructive	6 minutes	First Negative Speaker
4. Cross-Examination	3 minutes	Third Affirmative Speaker questions First Negative Speaker answers
5. First Affirmative Rebuttal	5 minutes	Second Affirmative Speaker
6. Cross-Examination	3 minutes	First Negative Speaker questions Second Affirmative Speaker answers
7. First Negative Rebuttal	5 minutes	Second Negative Speaker
8. Cross-Examination	3 minutes	First Affirmative Speaker questions Second Negative Speaker answers
9. Final Affirmative Rebuttal	5 minutes	Third Affirmative Speaker
10. Final Negative Rebuttal	5 minutes	Third Negative Speaker

REFUTATION AND REBUTTALS (TCO Q)

1. Explain that refutation is the most crucial element in the debate process because it is the way that one team tries to attack or respond to the other team's claims and arguments. To explain why refutation is important, use the following example. Tell the students that your favorite color is blue. Now ask them their favorite color. Explain that debate without refutation is about as exciting and meaningless as the exchange you just had. Without a chance to challenge a person's reasoning, evidence, and claims and demonstrate the superiority of your own, debate is purposeless. Emphasize that while it is important to attack the opponent's claim, evidence, and warrants during refutation, a debater must also offer a counter-argument that he or she can defend.

2. Describe the five steps in refuting a claim and write the name of each step on the board as you explain it. *(10 minutes)*

KEY POINTS

- The five steps in refuting a claim are the following:
    + Reference—Clearly state the argument you will be refuting
    + Response—Answer the opponent's argument by pointing out fallacies, inconsistencies, and problems in reasoning or evidence

- **Support**—If necessary, read, cite, or refer to evidence to justify, support, or prove your argument

- **Explanation**—Summarize your reasoning and evidence, and show how it overthrows your opponent's claims

- **Impact**— Show the implications of your argument by contrasting it with your opponents and explaining why yours is stronger

3. Write the following sentence on the board or use a proposition of your own:

   North Korea should give up its nuclear capabilities.

   Tell the students that they are currently engaged in a debate and that the sentence on the board is the stance of the opposing team. Prompt the participants to provide an appropriate reference, response, support, explanation, and impact to refute the opponent's reasoning, and write it next to the appropriate word on the board. *(10 minutes)*

4. Teach Activity 30: "Refutation Ball" (*DTW* p. 227). *(10 minutes)*

5. Explain that refutation is the process of responding to arguments and rebuttal is the formal speech that involves refutation.

6. Remind the students that rebuttals are the final speeches in the Karl Popper format and that the tasks of rebuttal speakers differ from those of the constructive speakers. Rebuttal speakers do not present new arguments; instead, they summarize their team's critical arguments, decide which of their team's arguments to advance, and explain the significance and implications of these arguments. *(10–15 minutes)*

KEY POINTS

Rebuttalists should do the following:

- **Summarize the most critical arguments and draw the judge's attention to how arguments have ended.** Rebuttal speakers must remember to draw the judge's attention to arguments their opponents have not refuted, because failure to address an argument means consent.

- **Identify vital issues.**

  - Identifying critical arguments that could cause their team to lose the debate, and responding appropriately.

  - Identifying critical arguments that could win the debate for their team, and highlighting them.

- Noting any relationships between vital arguments that highlight their case or negatively impact their opponents'.

- Determining whether an argument positively impacts their case.

- **Make choices.** Decide which arguments to advance and highlight. In making the decisions, debaters should consider time constraints (present the most important arguments first); the relative importance of various arguments (highlight the most important); and the judge's preferences.

- **Weigh implications.** Explain the significance and implications of their arguments by

    - addressing opposition arguments directly;

    - comparing and examining the merits of both teams' cases so that they can explain why their case is superior;

    - highlighting the key arguments an opponent fails to address so that they can claim that their position is stronger.

- **Plan your rebuttal speech** with a winning strategy in mind by:

    - thinking strategically and placing the most important arguments at the beginning of the speech;

    - planning in advance, paying careful attention to the arguments in the earlier speeches so that they can frame their speech as the debate progresses.

7. Teach Activity 31: "Developing Counterpoints" (*DTW* p. 227). *(15–20 minutes)*

8. Break *(10 minutes)*

Cross-examination (TCOs S & T)

1. Explain that the session will now focus on cross-examination—a period that typically has the most drama in a debate because debaters question and challenge each other's case directly. Emphasize that cross-examination is a courteous exchange of questions and answers. Thus, while this is the time to bring inconsistencies to light and question the other team's evidence, warrants, and claims, it is NOT a time to attack the other's position. Debaters must always be polite and respectful toward each other throughout the debate but especially during cross-examination. *(5 minutes)*

2. Explain that cross-examination is not meant merely to add drama to a debate. It has 10 specific purposes. Discuss why these are important and give examples for each. The 10 purposes are listed below. *(15 minutes)*

KEY POINTS

- The purpose of cross-examination is to accomplish the following:
    1. Obtain information
    2. Clarify an argument for the debater
    3. Clarify an argument for the judge
    4. Commit a debater to a position
    5. Gather information that could be useful in building arguments later in the debate
    6. Establish a plan of refutation
    7. Identify inadequacies in argument
    8. Undermine the opponent's credibility
    9. Enhance your own impression and credibility
    10. Prepare constructive arguments

3. Teach Activity 27: "Tag-Team Cross-Examination" (*DTW* p. 225). *(10 minutes)*

4. Teach Activity 28: "Secret Goal Cross-Examination" (*DTW* p. 225). *(10 minutes)*

5. Present the tips discussed in the text for making the most of questions and giving the best impression. Give examples of each from your experience. *(10 minutes)*

KEY POINTS

- Here are important tips to remember during cross-examination:
    + Ask questions; don't make speeches
    + Stay in control of the time and the questioning
    + Ask questions that pursue specific information
    + Remain flexible

- Direct questions toward specific goals
- Manage time appropriately
- Experiment with different tactics

6. Present the tips discussed in the textbook for making the most of responses and giving the best impression. Give examples of each from your experience. *(10 minutes)*

KEY POINTS

- Answer questions carefully, knowing that the questioner is usually trying to trap you into committing to a position, admitting an inconsistency, or exposing inadequacies in your case.
- Qualify answers to leading or unfair questions.
- Admit that you don't know an answer if you don't.

7. Explain that both the questioner and respondent must
    - be willing to commit the cross-examination period to a single crucial issue, rather than darting from issue to issue;
    - avoid capitulating too early in the cross-examination;
    - always connect the cross-examination to the broader issues in the debate.

    Illustrate each of these points with an example from your experience. *(5–7 minutes)*

8. Teach Activity 4: "Spar Debates" (*DTW* p. 210). *(20–25 minutes)*

Wrap-up

Briefly review this week's objectives and TCOs, and relate the activities and discussions from this class to each. Answer any remaining questions.

ADDITIONAL ACTIVITIES

Chapter 11:
    Activity 13: "Resolutional Analysis Worksheet" (*DTW* p. 216)
    Activity 33: "Refutation in Four Movements" (*DTW* p. 228)
    Activity 34: "Pick-up Rebuttal" (*DTW* p. 229)

Week 10

OBJECTIVES

Students will be able to do the following:

1. Understand how to arrange their speeches to the greatest advantage
2. Demonstrate and judge several components of verbal and nonverbal style
3. Recognize various elements of style useful in debate
4. Recognize the importance of appreciating and understanding a variety of cultures when debating internationally
5. Understand that they must surmount obstacles when debating internationally

CHAPTER FOCUS

DTW chapters 14 and 16

LESSON

WARM-UP

1. Teach Activity 39: "Delivery Warm-ups" (*DTW* p. 232). *(3–5 minutes)*
2. Teach Activity 40: "Articulation Drills'" (*DTW* p. 233). *(3–5 minutes)*

ARRANGEMENT, STYLE, AND DELIVERY (TCO U & V)

1. Explain that debaters must organize their speeches strategically. Typically, they begin with an overview of how they will proceed. They then present their arguments, starting with the strongest. As the debate develops, they continue to summarize very briefly where they are in the debate and what the audience can next expect.
2. Explain that there are four common ways to organize a debate. As you discuss each, provide examples from your experience. *(15–20 minutes)*

KEY POINTS

Debates can be arranged by the following:

- **Topic, using the folllowing approaches:**
  + Organize by definition—formulate that speech around how a word or phrase is defined
  + Organize by cause—frame a speech around a causal connection
  + Organize by reason—construct a speech around multiple reasons to support or reject an issue
  + Organize by question and answer—assume the proposition is a vital question and frame the speech around answers to the question
- **Time/history**—describing a controversial issue, discussing the issue's relevance to contemporary society, and offering a view of the world after the issue is settled
- **Problem-solution**—articulating a problem, proposing a solution, and presenting the merits of the solution
- **Relationship**—linking ideas that are posed

3. Discuss the various components of style and delivery. Students often have difficulty understanding these by just reading a textbook. Therefore, you should illustrate each component, providing examples of both good and bad style. *(10–15 minutes)*

KEY POINTS

Key components of style are these:

- **Clarity**—the speaker's precision of thought and speech
- **Eloquence**—the debater's ability to speak fluently and persuasively
- **Accuracy**—the debater's ability to say what he or she means
- **Vocal clutter**—the debater's ability to speak without unnecessary sounds ("umms")
- **Pitch**—the debater's ability to properly marry pitch to emotion
- **Rate**—the debater's ability to deliver a speech at a rate slightly faster than normal speech

- **Volume**—the speaker's ability to change volume for variety and emphasis

4. You might want to expand the discussion on the components of style by asking for a volunteer to give an impromptu 3- to 5-minute speech on how to start and drive a car. Tell the volunteer that the class will evaluate how she used the seven components of style. Write the components on the board. After the volunteer has presented her speech, ask the class to help you judge each component on a scale of 1 to 10. Ask for another volunteer and repeat the process. You may give him the same topic or assign another, such as how to iron a shirt. Continue until all students have a good understanding of the components. *(10–15 minutes)*

5. Teach Activity 32: "Repetition, Assertion, and Deviation" (*DTW* p. 228). *(30 minutes)*

6. Discuss the elements of style students can use to present their arguments in a meaningful and powerful way and provide examples of each. *(10–15 minutes)*

KEY POINTS

Key elements of style include the following:

- **Alliteration**—repetition of beginning consonants in words
- **Allusion**—a shared historical or cultural reference
- **Hyperbole**—an extreme exaggeration
- **Metaphors and analogies**—comparing one thing or event to another
- **Personifications**—attributing human qualities to inanimate objects
- **Repetition**—repeating a word or phrase for emphasis or entertainment
- **Declarative sentences**—makes an argument more powerful

7. Remind students that the nonverbal elements of style—facial expressions, gestures, and eye contact—are integral parts of good public speaking. Give examples of both the appropriate and inappropriate use of these elements. Remind students that nonverbal language is closely associated with culture, and that they must learn what is appropriate when debating in an international setting. *(10 minutes)*

8. Break *(10 minutes)*

DEBATING IN AN INTERNATIONAL SETTING (TCO X)

1. Begin with the following game, which uncovers stereotypes and shows how silly or unfounded these are. Note that the stereotypes are offensive (this is the point of the game—to help to neutralize any offensive stereotypes participants may bring to the collective table) and are written with an American audience in mind. You will need to adjust the stereotypes to reflect those common among your students. *(20 minutes)*

   A. Write commonly held stereotypes on small strips of paper. Write one statement for every two students you have. Here are some examples for an American audience:

   - Mexicans are lazy because they won't learn English.
   - Republicans are far-right Christian warmongers.
   - Muslims are terrorists.
   - Southerners are ignorant.
   - Blacks are welfare recipients.

   B. Now cut the sentence strips so that the racial or cultural group is separated from the stereotyped action. For example, in cutting the first stereotype sentence above, you would have a strip that says "Mexicans" and another that says "are lazy because they won't learn English."

   C. Distribute one piece to each student. Tell them that they have one half of a commonly held stereotype and that they must find the student that has the matching half. Tell them that they have 3 minutes to find their match.

   D. Once the students have found their matches, ask each pair to stand up and read the stereotype. Note that participants may be embarrassed and may feel that they will be seen as racist for even acknowledging that these stereotypes exist. After the stereotype matches are read, ask the students if they know of any other stereotypes. Prompt participants for reasons why some of these stereotypes or racial slurs exist. Remind them that the best way to tear down a stereotype is to analyze it and bust the myth or the trepidation that surrounds it. Be wary of doing this final step with students—they may not be mature enough to handle the subject matter respectfully.

2. Discuss how debate is a great equalizer as people from different backgrounds and cultures gather to examine issues and share ideas in open forum. Emphasize that those participating in international debate must accept cultural diversity and be aware and respectful of other cultures in all interactions. *(5–10 minutes)*

3. Teach Activity 37: "Subversive Rewriting" (*DTW* p. 231). *(15 minutes)*

4. Remind the students that Karl Popper debates are in English and explain that this presents a major challenge to non-native English speakers. Explore some of the challenges with the students. Ask them how they would feel if they had to debate in a language they were learning, knowing that they would be judged on how they performed. *(10–15 minutes)*

5. Reiterate that in order to avoid being rude or discourteous, debaters must learn about differences in etiquette and customs.

Wrap-up

Briefly review this week's objectives and TCOs, and relate the activities and discussions from this class to each. Answer any remaining questions. *(3 minutes)*

ADDITIONAL ACTIVITIES

Chapter 14:
    Activity 6: "Argument Assembly" (*DTW* p. 212)
    Activity 35: "Rebuttal 'Re-gives'" (*DTW* p. 230)
    Activity 36: "Oral Style" (*DTW* p. 231)
    Activity 41: "Emphasis Drills" (*DTW* p. 233)

Week 11

OBJECTIVES

Students will be able to do the following:

1. Understand and appreciate the responsibilities of debate judges

2. Flow and judge a debate and explain their decisions in oral and written form

CHAPTER FOCUS

DTW chapter 15

PREPARATION

Obtain sample written or videotaped debates. The latter would be better because they would allow participants to judge verbal and nonverbal presentation. Any formal debate will do—the Karl Popper format would be ideal, and student debates captured on film would be great, but presidential debates will suffice if you cannot locate anything else.

LESSON

Warm-up

Explain that this week the students will step out of the role of debater and focus on the role of judge. Review the objectives from the prior weeks and remind the students that they need to keep these in mind as they switch roles. *(5–10 minutes)*

Judging Debates (TCO W)

1. Explain that the primary responsibility of the judge is to determine which team has done the better job of debating. Judges do so by concentrating on the arguments presented. They must not let personal bias or opinion or knowledge of the subject influence their decisions. Judges must offer an explanation for why and how they made their decisions. *(15 minutes)*

KEY POINTS

- Judges must focus only on what is presented or argued in the debate.

- Judges must not let personal opinions and biases or prior knowledge of the topic influence them.

- Judges must decide a debate based on which team was more persuasive in its arguments.

- Judges must make their decisions independently, without any discussion either with other judges or others present at the debate.

- Judges must explain their decisions to the participants. They should be able to explain the main issues in the debate, how the winning team proved to be more persuasive, and what the losing side did that cost it the debate.

- Judges must be impartial and objective.

2. Discuss a judge's other responsibilities, including timekeeping, maintaining a positive climate in the debate hall, taking notes or keeping a flow sheet of the debate, providing written comments on a judging ballot, and providing an oral explanation of the decision. *(5 minutes)*

3. Break *(10 minutes)*

4. Review with the students the skill of flowing a debate they learned in Week 5. Explain that they will now take that skill a step further by learning how to assign points to teams as a judge would do. (You can use the following point assignments as a guide, or you may alter the points as you see appropriate.) Explain that judges typically assign 20–30 points to each speaker based on the arguments offered, and how well the speaker presented his speech and responded to the other team's arguments. Rarely does a speaker receive less than 19 points; just as it is rare for a speaker to score more than 27 points. Consequently, judges need to be very exacting with their point assignments and ensure that points given are well earned. Note that the following descriptions are a matter of semantics and you may wish to provide more exact guidelines for each point value or have the students come up with some. The following is a sample of points and descriptions for each point value.

19.	There are a number of blatant flaws in presentation—overall a poor job
20.	Acceptable but contains a few major problems
21.	The effort at doing a good job was made but not well done for the most part
22.	Just below average
23.	Simply an average speech—there were no blatant errors or glaring problems
24.	Decent speech but simply just above average
25.	Overall a good speech with excellence in only one area
26.	Very good speech; with presenters articulate and providing intelligent presentations
27.	Excellent speech with exceptional delivery and analysis
28.	Phenomenal speech; leaves a solid, lasting impression
29.	Absolutely tremendous, close to flawless speech
30.	Rarely given point award—reserved for truly once-in-a-lifetime speeches

After each speaker has received his or her total points, the judges add the points earned for the speakers on each team together. The team with the most points wins the debate.

5. Explain that you will now show a videotape of an actual debate and the students will be serving as judges of the debate. They will flow the debate and award points. Distribute blank copies of the Argument Flow Sheet (p. 90) and Karl Popper Debate Ballot (p. 91)—enough for each participant to have several of each. Review each and answer any questions the students have about the forms or the process. Then show the taped debate. *(60–90 minutes total)*

6. After the students have finished, draw a sample flow sheet on the board and prompt the class to fill it out with you so that all students can see how they fared in flowing the debate. Correct where necessary and allow participants to make a fresh flow sheet based on your corrections, if they wish. Now ask them who won the debate and why. Ask them to share their comments from their ballots. Be sure that the students explain their rationale for deciding the winner and that their reasoning is appropriate. *(30 minutes)*

7. If you wish, use Activity 48: "Video Judging" (*DTW* p. 240) to expand this lesson.

Wrap-up

Briefly review this week's objectives and TCOs, and relate the activities and discussions from this class to each. Answer any remaining questions. *(3 minutes)*

ADDITIONAL ACTIVITIES

Chapter 15:
- Activity 20: "Flowing the News" (*DTW* p. 219)
- Activity 21: "Post-debate Assessment" (*DTW* p. 220)
- Activity 49: "Shadow Judging" (*DTW* p. 241)

Week 12

OBJECTIVES

Students will be able to do the following:

1. Demonstrate what they have learned about argumentation for debaters

2. Construct and refute arguments in the Karl Popper debate format

3. Demonstrate debating skills in a debate setting

4. Judge a debate using a flow chart and point sheet

5. Understand their role in promoting debate as an educational methodology

LESSON

WARM-UP

Greet the class and explain that this final session will be spent discussing, evaluating, and demonstrating concepts they have learned in the preceding sessions. As a cumulative assessment piece, there will be up to three debates held concurrently in this session. (Note that this is based on the assumption that you have 27 students in your class with three different groups holding a debate in various areas of the room at the same time. If you have fewer than 27 students, you may choose to have only two debates. If you have many more than 27 students, you can increase the number of debates. If you have a number of students that is not divisible by 9, you can deal with the odd numbers by having no less than 2 judges but as many additional judges as you feel are appropriate.

Explain that every student will participate in a debate—as an affirmative team member, a negative team member, or a judge. Each debate group will hold its debate in a different area of the classroom, and you will move between groups to observe. Explain that this final session will also include time for feedback, questions, and an overall wrap-up of the course. (*5 minutes*)

FINAL CLASS SESSION

1. Assign the roles of three affirmative team members, three negative team members, and three judges to each debate group. Ask students to physically gather in their groups before you continue. Answer any questions before continuing. (10 minutes)

2. Once students are assembled in their groups, review the rules of the Karl Popper debate format. Remind the students of the time limits for each section of the debate, the amount of time each team has for discussion and preparation, and the proper protocol for debaters. Distribute copies of the Argument Flow Sheet (p. 90) and Karl Popper Debate Ballot and Scoring Rubric (p. 91) to all participants and review the scoring procedures. Make sure that there are extra copies of both sheets. Answer any remaining questions. *(5 minutes)*

3. Announce the topic of the debate. It should be one the class did not already use in the course. Once you have announced the topic, tell the affirmative and negative teams that they have 10 minutes to prepare before the official start of the debates. As the teams prepare, call the judges over and review the accepted point system and the procedures for flowing a debate. Answer any questions they may have. Also explain timing procedures and ensure that the judges have a timepiece to keep accurate time. After the 10 minutes have passed, ask the judges to return to their groups and help their teams to arrange the chairs and desks for the debate. *(10 minutes)*

4. When everyone is ready, announce that the debate has now begun. Allow the debate to proceed according to format, and move between the debate groups as an unofficial judge so that you can give feedback to the debaters and judges. *(52 minutes)*

5. When the debate ends, ask the groups to turn their desks and chairs toward the center of the room. Starting with the first debate group, ask the judges to summarize the flow of the debate they just watched. Then ask the affirmative and negative teams if they feel that the flow was accurate, and if so, give thumbs up. If they think that it was not accurate, they should give thumbs down and explain how they might have relayed their message better. Note that at this point, the judges have not yet announced the scores or the winner of the debate. Once the speakers have had their say, the judges should announce the scores and winners and justify their decisions. Highlight any concerns you may have with their scoring techniques or explanations and ask each judge how she felt about giving scores and how confident she was in her decisions. Draw attention to any vast differences in scoring among the judges and ask the class how this may have happened. Continue this procedure with each debate group. *(20–30 minutes)*

6. After the groups have completed their reviews, ask the class for feedback on their experiences as debaters and judges. *(7 minutes)*

    - Which was the easiest role?
    - Which was the most difficult role?
    - Did you think you had enough time to prepare?

- Did you and your teammates work as a team rather than as three individuals? How did this affect the team's performance?

Wrap-up

Review the terminal course objectives and highlight the activities throughout the course that achieved these TCOs. Also review the course syllabus and highlight how the course fulfilled each component. *(10–15 minutes)*

Appendix

Course Syllabus

DESCRIPTION

This course introduces you to argumentation and to the practical skills needed for debate, specifically, using the Karl Popper debate format. The three broad topics covered are argumentation theory, argument construction, and debating skills.

REQUIRED READING

Trapp, Robert, Joseph P. Zompetti, Jurate Motiejunaite, and William Driscoll. *Discovering the World through Debate*. 3rd ed. New York: International Debate Education Association, 2005.

COURSE REQUIREMENTS

1. Assigned Readings—Each lesson will include assigned readings from *Discovering the World through Debate*, third edition. You should complete the readings before the session so that you can gain the maximum benefit from the lesson.

2. Debate Analysis—You will analyze at least two Karl Popper debates using an argument flow sheet.

3. Debate Design and Delivery—You will design and deliver a structured debate and will also assume the various roles that debaters take in actual debates.

4. In-Class Projects—In-class projects and impromptu debate sessions will help you learn how debates are structured and how to participate in debates. They will also help you understand the demands and expectations of debate judges.

5. Class Participation—Because this is a practical course, you are expected to actively participate in debates and in-class discussions and activities.

6. Assessment—You will be assessed on your participation and performance in debates as an individual and as part of a team. You are expected to attend class regularly.

TERMINAL COURSE OBJECTIVES (TCOS)

Terminal Course Objectives (TCOs) are the main learning objectives that students taking the course should meet. These objectives explain what you should know or be able to do by the end of the course.

A. Given the important elements of argument, define and properly utilize claims, evidence, warrants, and reservations.

B. Given a model to simulate a theoretical argument, appropriately chart out an argument to ensure all necessary parts are included.

C. Given evidence and a claim, assess the structure of an argument as simple, convergent, or independent.

D. Given a claim or proposition, evaluate whether it is a claim of definition, description, relationship, or evaluation.

E. Given evidence for a claim, categorize it as reality-based or preference-based or a combination of reality- and preference-based.

F. Given a value hierarchy, categorize whether to use evidence as quantity, quality, order, existent, essence, or person.

G. Given an argumentative warrant, categorize as example, analogy, causal warrant, authority, principle, incompatibility, or disassociation, or some combination of these warrants, by its use in an argument.

H. Given a criterion for logical assessment of an argument, assess if the standards of acceptability, relevance, and sufficiency are met.

I. Given a fallacy, identify how it fails to meet a criterion for logical assessment of an argument.

J. Given an example of a Karl Popper debate, devise or analyze a debate within the established format.

K. Given the claim of an argument, classify it as a cause-and-effect, value, or policy claim.

L. Given an argument to defend or attack, apply the five steps of refutation to a debate.

M. Given a debate topic, develop a plan to generate general and specific knowledge.

N. Given an opportunity to cross-examine the other team, question the opponent appropriately, flexibly, pointedly, specifically, and with innovation when necessary.

O. Given the opportunity to respond to cross-examination, respond carefully, succinctly, and appropriately, and if necessary, admit lack of knowledge.

P. Given a debate topic, arrange ideas by topic, time and history, problem and solution, or relationship.

Q. Given components and elements of style, exhibit and identify those related to the use of language, voice, speech style, and nonverbal style.

R. Given the opportunity to serve as a debate judge, understand the criteria for judging and ethically carry out the duties and tasks required.

S. Given the requirements of debating internationally, understand and exhibit the demands required of debaters arguing within the confines of foreign languages, countries, and customs.

T. Given the benefits of debating clubs in schools, devise ways to foster support, inclusion, and cooperation.

U. Given an opportunity to read or hear a debate, flow the debate using appropriate columns and references.

Worksheet 1

DISTINGUISHING BETWEEN CLAIMS, PROPOSITIONS, AND EVIDENCE

Each of the blank models below should represent the argument as labeled. Use the statements on the second page of the activity as the evidence, claims, and propositions for each debate topic. Write each statement in its appropriate blank on the model. Be prepared to explain why you placed each statement where you did.

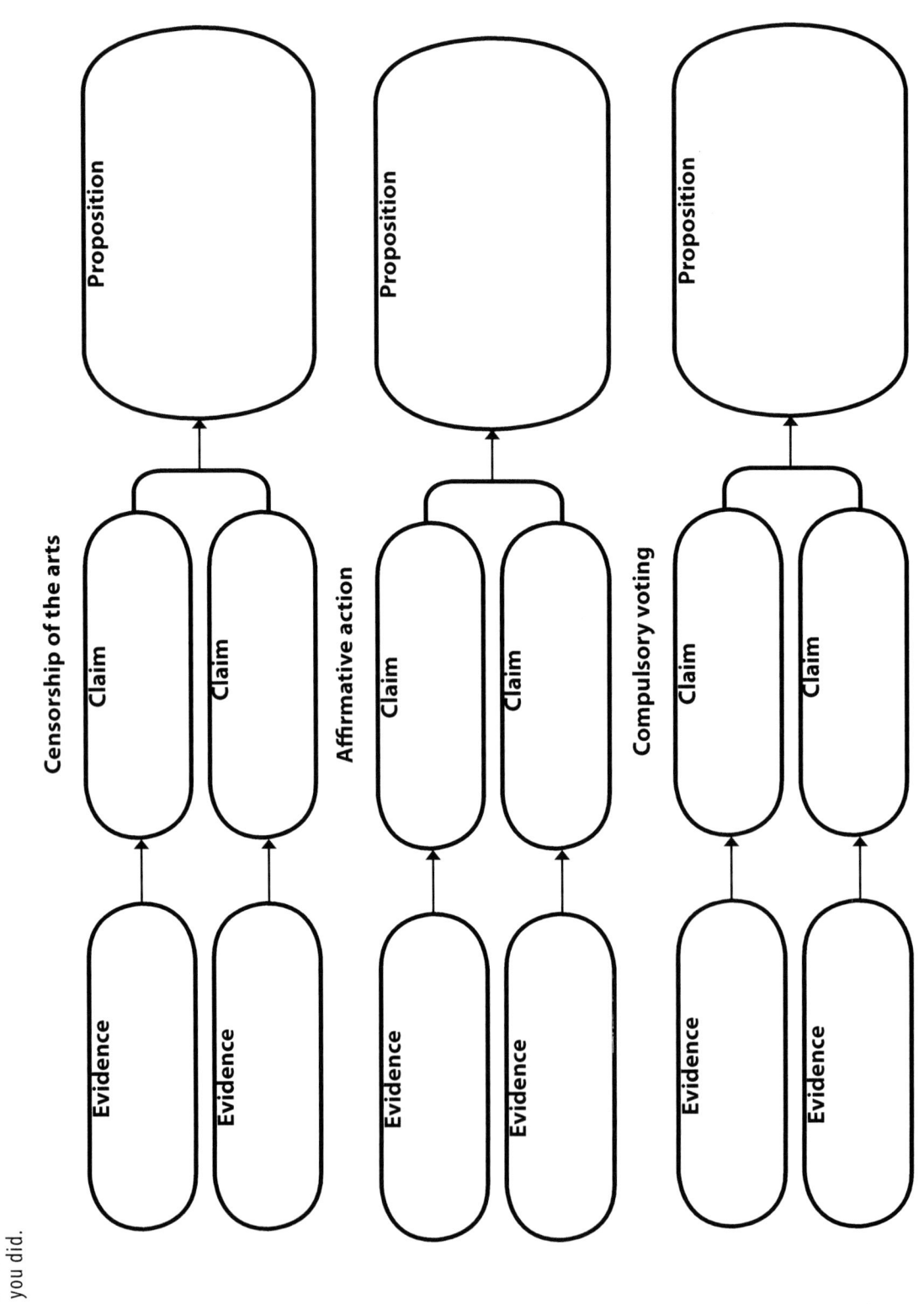

Censorship of the arts

Evidence → Claim ↘
                    Proposition
Evidence → Claim ↗

Affirmative action

Evidence → Claim ↘
                    Proposition
Evidence → Claim ↗

Compulsory voting

Evidence → Claim ↘
                    Proposition
Evidence → Claim ↗

STATEMENTS

- Throughout history, many people have died for the right to freely elect their own government.
- Freedom of artistic expression should have limits.
- Females and minorities do not have equal access to employment and education.
- Affirmative action levels the playing field for under-represented groups.
- Slander is a limitation on freedom of speech and is justified.
- The government should ensure that art is acceptable for all audiences.
- The majority of top jobs are held by white males.
- The government sends a message by what it allows in society.
- Work that is potentially offensive is not considered art—art should be enjoyed by all.
- The right not to vote is as fundamental as the right to vote.
- Hiring only white males is discriminatory.
- Living in a free society allows various kinds of freedoms.
- Making informed decisions at the ballot box is important.
- People forced to vote will not make educated decisions.
- Discrimination is bad and creates conflict.

Worksheet 2

Karl Popper Quotes

"You cannot have a rational discussion with a man who prefers shooting you to being convinced by you."

". . . it seems to me certain that more people are killed out of righteous stupidity than out of wickedness."

"We all remember how many religious wars were fought for a religion of love and gentleness; how many bodies were burned alive with the genuinely kind intention of saving souls from the eternal fire of hell."

"Do not allow your dreams of a beautiful world to lure you away from the claims of men who suffer here and now. Our fellow men have a claim to our help; no generation must be sacrificed for the sake of future generations."

"Leadership is solving problems. The day soldiers stop bringing you their problems is the day you have stopped leading them. They have either lost confidence that you can help or concluded you do not care. Either case is a failure of leadership."

"The belief in a political Utopia is especially dangerous. This is possibly connected with the fact that the search for a better world, like the investigation of our environment, is (if I am correct) one of the oldest and most important of all the instincts."

"When we enter a new situation in life and are confronted by a new person, we bring with us the prejudices of the past and our previous experiences of people. These prejudices we project upon the new person. Indeed, getting to know a person is largely a matter of withdrawing projections; of dispelling the smoke screen of what we imagine he is like and replacing it with the reality of what he is actually like."

"It is often asserted that discussion is only possible between people who have a common language and accept common basic assumptions. I think that this is a mistake. All that is needed is a readiness to learn from one's partner in the discussion, which includes a genuine wish to understand what he intends to say. If this readiness is there, the discussion on righteous stupidity will be the more fruitful the more the partner's backgrounds differ."

"Why do I think that we, the intellectuals, are able to help? Simply because we, the intellectuals, have done the most terrible harm for thousands of years. Mass murder in the name of an idea, a doctrine, a theory, a religion—that is all 'our' doing, 'our' invention: the invention of the intellectuals. If only we would stop setting man against man—often with the best intentions—much would be gained. Nobody can say that it is impossible for us to stop doing this."

"Before we as individuals are even conscious of our existence we have been profoundly influenced for a considerable time (since before birth) by our relationship to other individuals who have complicated histories, and are members of a society which has an infinitely more complicated and longer history than they do (and are members of it at a particular time and place in that history); and by the time we are able to make conscious choices we are already making use of categories in a language which has reached a particular degree of development through the lives of countless generations of human beings before us. . . . We are social creatures to the inmost centre of our being. The notion that one can begin anything at all from scratch, free from the past, or unindebted to others, could not conceivably be more wrong."

Worksheet 3

Group Discussion Questions for Karl Popper Debate Transcript and Commentary Reading

FIRST AFFIRMATIVE

1. What is the purpose of this speech?

2. Each group member should give an example of a stronger introductory remark that Asa could have made.

3. Each group member should give an example of what Asa could have said to preempt a negative argument about individual countries stopping human trafficking.

4. How else could Asa have improved her first affirmative speech?

FIRST AFFIRMATIVE CROSS-EXAMINATION

1. What is the purpose of this section?

2. Who is involved in this section?

3. Give examples of politeness offered in the debate.

4. Each group member should give an example of a stronger response that Asa could give to Baya's first two questions.

5. Baya is said to be laying the groundwork for the negative strategy. What is the strategy, based on this section?

NEGATIVE CONSTRUCTION AND REFUTATION

1. What is the purpose of this section?

2. Who is involved in this section?

3. What is negative's stance on the proposition?

4. Each group member should give an example of evidence that Jon could use to support the claims that the ICC would violate foreign sovereignty and would become corrupt.

78 | Teacher's guide for Discovering the world through DEBATE

5. Does John effectively support the statement that violations of sovereignty caused WWI and WWII? Explain.

CROSS-EXAMINATION

1. What is the purpose of this section?
2. Who is involved in this section?
3. How do you think this section would be different if Jon did not have knowledge of what the Nuremburg trials were?
4. Who do you think was a stronger debater in this section? Why?
5. Are there any further points that Sergejs could have made to Jon?
6. Did Jon defend his team's position well? If not, how would you improve it?

AFFIRMATIVE REBUTTAL AND REFUTATION

1. What is the purpose of this section?
2. Who is involved in this section?
3. Why does Peguy thank the negative team?
4. Peguy refers to several pieces of evidence submitted by the negative team. Why does he do this? Does it undermine the affirmative's position? Why or why not?
5. Each group member should give a historical example that Peguy could use in his speech.

SECOND NEGATIVE CROSS-EXAMINATION

1. What is the purpose of this section?
2. Who is involved in this section?
3. How well does Peguy respond to Jon's assertion that the ICC would not adequately represent the position of all nations? Give an example of how he could have responded.
4. Each group member should give an example of how Jon, in his response to the affirmative team, could have better used Peguy's statement in his earlier speech that sovereignty was bad.
5. What does Jon mean by "a fallacy relying on historic tradition"?
6. Both debaters continue to interrupt each other. Is this acceptable debate etiquette? Why or why not?

SECOND NEGATIVE SPEECH

1. What is the purpose of this section?

2. Who is involved in this section?

3. Has Alex responded to all evidence and propositions that the affirmative has proposed?

4. What kind of evidence should Alex give to support his team's assertions that the ICC will be discriminatory and that sovereignty would be violated? Each group member should give an example of evidence that could be presented.

5. Each group member should give an example of how Alex's speech could have been stronger?

SECOND AFFIRMATIVE CROSS-EXAMINATION

1. What is the purpose of this section?

2. Who is involved in this section?

3. Asa asks many questions at once, confusing Alex. Do you think that this tactic makes Asa look hurried and unfocused or Alex seem overwhelmed? How could her questioning be improved, OR how could Alex better respond to Asa's questioning?

4. How do Asa's questions about jurisdiction confuse Alex? What is your take on his response? Give an example of how Alex could better field these questions.

THIRD AFFIRMATIVE SPEECH

1. What is the purpose of this section?

2. Who is involved in this section?

3. Each group member should give an example of how Sergejs could use the concessions that Asa gained from negative in the previous section in this speech.

4. Each group member should give an example of how Sergejs could better respond to negative's concerns about the ICC.

5. Has affirmative responded sufficiently to all concerns that the negative asserted regarding the ICC in the beginning of the debate?

6. If not, what points were not responded to?

THIRD NEGATIVE SPEECH

1. What is the purpose of this section?

2. Who is involved in this section?

3. Why has Baya not responded to Asa's suggestion that both negative's and affirmative's proposals (the ICC **and** national policies) could help to curb the problem?

4. Each group member should give an example of how Baya could respond to Asa's suggestion in the previous section.

5. Has negative responded sufficiently to all concerns that the affirmative asserted regarding national policies in the beginning of the debate?

6. If not, what points were not responded to?

OVERALL

Each group member should give a "gut reaction" to the debate and decide which team won the argument and why.

Worksheet 4

Arguing and Refuting Causal Relationships

Directions: Use the paragraph below to demonstrate the different methods for showing cause and effect between the evidence and the claim—method of agreement, method of difference, method of correlation—and demonstrate the three elements necessary in constructing a cause-and-effect argument.

EVIDENCE

Over 500 people ate at Café Eats, a new restaurant, on New Year's Eve. Three people from three different parties eating at Café Eats that night came down with food poisoning. All three people called the manager, Mr. Eats, the next day to tell him that they think they contracted food poisoning at his restaurant, and demanded restitution. He asked each of them what they ate that night. The first had chicken soup, coleslaw, a cola, a steak, and a piece of New Year's Eve cake; the second had cream of chicken soup, a salad, a chicken sandwich, coleslaw, and an iced tea; the third consumed Chinese chicken soup, a salad, coleslaw, the fish special, and a lemonade.

CLAIM

The coleslaw served at Café Eats caused the three to contract food poisoning.

Affirmative: Using the method of agreement, structure an argument that the coleslaw caused the three to contract food poisoning.

Negative: Using the method of agreement, structure an argument that the coleslaw did not cause the three to contract food poisoning.

Affirmative: Using the method of difference, structure an argument that the coleslaw caused the three to contract food poisoning.

Negative: Using the method of difference, structure an argument that the coleslaw did not cause the three to contract food poisoning.

Affirmative: Using the method of correlation, structure an argument that the coleslaw caused the three to contract food poisoning.

Negative: Using the method of correlation, structure an argument that the coleslaw did not cause the three to contract food poisoning.

Worksheet 5

Building a Case for and against a Simple Value Proposition

PART 1: BUILDING A CASE FOR A SIMPLE VALUE PROPOSITION

Directions: Read the passage below about how AIDS affects children. After reading the passage, complete the outline to build a case for the simple value proposition given.

> When HIV/AIDS enters a household by infecting one or both parents, the very fabric of a child's life falls apart. The statistics are numbing: by 2003, 15 million children under the age of 18 had been orphaned by HIV/AIDS; just two years earlier, the figure stood at 11.5 million.[1] Eight out of 10 of these children live in sub-Saharan Africa. It is estimated that in 2010, over 18 million African children under the age of 18 will have lost one or both parents to HIV/AIDS, and the number of double orphans—children whose mother and father have died—will increase by about 2 million over the same period.[2] Millions more live in households with sick and dying family members. Although they are not yet orphaned, these children also suffer the pernicious effects of HIV/AIDS.
>
> (*Source:* UNICEF, The State of the World's Children Report, 2005.)

NOTES

1. World Health Organization, The World Health Report 2004, Geneva, 2004, p. 2; and Joint United Nations Programme on HIV/AIDS, 2004 Report on the Global AIDS Epidemic, op. cit., p. 30.
2. Joint United Nations Programme on HIV/AIDS, United Nations Children's Fund and the United States Agency for International Development, Children on the Brink 2004, op. cit., p. 10.

I. Introduction

    A. Statement of the proposition: Children do not need to have HIV/AIDS to be devastated by it.

    B. Definition of terms _____

    _____

II. Argument

    A. AIDS affects more than the actual people who are infected with HIV.

        1. (Description)_____

        _____

        2. (Relationship)_____

        _____

        3. (Evaluation) _____

        _____

III. Conclusion

    _____
    _____
    _____

On the back of this sheet, make your case stronger by adding presence to the value.

PART 2: CONSTRUCTING AN ARGUMENT TO OPPOSE A VALUE PROPOSITION

<u>Directions:</u> Re-read the previous passage about how AIDS affects children. After reading the passage, refer back to your responses in the outline to build an affirmative case for the simple value proposition given. Below, build a negative case on the points that affirmative presented, and if you choose, build an argument that is independent of any points presented by affirmative.

I. Negative's Opposing Argument:

_____
_____

A. (Description) _____
_____

B. (Relationship) _____
_____

C. (Evaluation) _____
_____

II. Optional (but highly recommended) Independent Argument:

_____
_____

A. (Description) _____
_____

B. (Relationship) _____
_____

C. (Evaluation) _____
_____

Worksheet 6 ●

Building a Case for a Comparative Value Proposition - Fact Sheet

<u>Directions:</u> Read the fact sheet about the feminization of AIDS. With a partner, complete the outline to build a case for a comparative value proposition based on the reading.

At the outset of the HIV/AIDS pandemic in the early 1980s, men greatly outnumbered women among those who were HIV-positive. Since then, the proportion of women with HIV has risen steadily; today, nearly half of those who are HIV-positive are women or girls. The pandemic's "feminization" is most apparent in sub-Saharan Africa, where close to 60 percent of those who are HIV-positive are female; among young people aged 15–24 in the region, females account for 75 percent of the infected population.

Poverty and gender inequality are the driving forces behind the fact that the spread and impact of the HIV/AIDS pandemic disproportionately affect women. Faced with economic hardship, women and girls become more vulnerable to prostitution and sex trafficking, in which they have little power to negotiate safe sex. They may also succumb to the lure of transactional sex, entering into relationships with older or wealthier men in exchange for money, goods, and other basic services. This transactional sex greatly increases their risk of contracting HIV.

Violence against women, deeply embedded in some of the countries most affected by HIV/AIDS, as well as social taboos that foster a culture of silence around sex and the risk of HIV transmission, increase the risk of women and girls becoming infected with HIV. In addition, women are more physically susceptible to HIV infection than men: male-to-female transmission during sex is about twice as likely as female-to-male transmission.

Higher rates of HIV/AIDS among women have changed the pattern of orphaning in sub-Saharan Africa, with maternal orphans due to HIV/AIDS now outnumbering paternal orphans due to HIV/AIDS. In the most-affected countries in sub-Saharan Africa, 60 percent of all orphans have lost their mother, compared with 40 percent in Asia and Latin America and the Caribbean. Although the implications of a child losing her or his mother as compared to her or his father are still not fully understood, recent household surveys show that in the countries of southern Africa, maternal orphans are especially likely to be "virtual" double orphans, as it is common for the father to live elsewhere.

Besides forming the majority of those infected, women and girls bear the brunt of the pandemic in other ways. In many countries women are the caretakers and guardians of family life. When family members become ill, it is the women in the family who take care of them. This burden of care is far reaching and not age-specific. In families where assistance is needed to tend for sick relatives or to compensate for a loss of income, girls tend to be the first to be withdrawn from school. This not only deals a devastating blow to their education, it also prevents them from obtaining vital information about HIV/AIDS prevention and transmission, and therefore increases the risk that they will become infected. Older women also shoulder the burden of care as their adult children fall ill, and often die, from HIV/AIDS. And as the pandemic claims more lives, it is these women who, increasingly often, are left to take care of children orphaned by HIV/AIDS.

When the main income provider falls ill or dies, the remaining caregivers have to contend with additional work and diminished incomes and assets. Women are often responsible for providing the family's food and shelter, and may not be able to manage on their meager earnings. As a result, some are driven to transactional sex in exchange for food and other essential goods. As HIV/AIDS claims the lives of their husbands, fathers, and brothers, women—especially those in cultures where property rights devolve along the male line—also face losing the family land and property.

Women can also be primary targets of the stigma that is attached to HIV/AIDS. Women are often the first to be tested for HIV and blamed for introducing the disease into the household or community, even though their male partners may have been the true source of the infection. There is growing evidence that HIV/AIDS can incite violence as women face retribution for their HIV-positive status. The fear of such violence causes some women and girls to avoid getting tested or seeking treatment if infected. Lower rates of employment among women also mean that they may encounter difficulties in obtaining private medical insurance or paying for treatment.

Given that gender inequality is one of the main causes of the dramatic increase in the number of women infected by HIV/AIDS, gender-sensitive approaches are key when designing prevention programs. Women need to have access to the knowledge and tools that will help them protect themselves from becoming infected. Women should constitute at least half of the millions in developing countries expected to gain access to antiretroviral therapy in the coming years. Communities need to remove barriers that prevent or

hinder women from being tested, including the risk of violence they may face if they are found to be HIV-positive.

(*Source:* **UNICEF, The State of the World's Children Report: 2005.)**

I. Introduction

   A. Statement of the proposition: _____
   _____

   B. Definition of terms _____
   _____

II. Arguments

   A. _____
   _____

      1. (Description)_____
      _____

      2. (Relationship)_____
      _____

      3. (Evaluation) _____
      _____

   B. _____
   _____

      1. (Description)_____
      _____

      2. (Relationship)_____
      _____

      3. (Evaluation) _____
      _____

   C. _____
   _____

      1. (Description)_____
      _____

      2. (Relationship)_____
      _____

      3. (Evaluation) _____
      _____

III. Conclusion

   _____
   _____

On the back of this sheet, make your case stronger by adding presence to the value.

Worksheet 6 / Building a Case for a Comparative Value Proposition - Fact Sheet

Worksheet 7
Argument Flow Sheet

Argument Flow Sheet

First affirmative	First negative	Second affirmative	Second negative	Third affirmative	Third negative

Karl Popper Debate Ballot and Scoring Rubric

Karl Popper Debate Ballot

Affirmative Team				Negative Team		
	1A	2A	3A	1N	2N	3N
Name						
Points						
Rank						

Affirmative Comments	Negative Comments

The team that did a better job in debating the topic was _____

Judge's signature: _____

Worksheet 8 / Karl Popper Debate Ballot and Scoring Rubric | 91

Karl Popper Scoring Rubric

19.	There are a number of blatant flaws in presentation—overall a poor job
20.	Acceptable but contains a few major problems
21.	The effort at doing a good job was made but not well done for the most part
22.	Just below average
23.	Simply an average speech—there were no blatant errors or glaring problems
24.	Decent speech but simply just above average
25.	Overall a good speech with excellence in only one area
26.	Very good speech; with presenters articulate and providing intelligent presentations
27.	Excellent speech with exceptional delivery and analysis
28.	Phenomenal speech; leaves a solid, lasting impression
29.	Absolutely tremendous, close to flawless speech
30.	Rarely given point award—reserved for truly once-in-a-lifetime speeches